W9-AHN-402

Michael Symon's

CARNIVORE

MICHAEL SYMON'S CARNIVORE

120 RECIPES FOR MEAT LOVERS

MICHAEL SYMON

WITH
DOUGLAS TRATTNER

PHOTOGRAPHS BY JENNIFER MAY

CLARKSON POTTER/PUBLISHERS

NEW YORK

Published in the United States by Clarkson Potter/
Publishers, an imprint of the Crown Publishing Group, a
division of Random House, Inc., New York.
www.crownpublishing.com
www.clarksonpotter.com

CLARKSON POTTER is a trademark and POTTER with
colophon is a registered trademark of Random House, Inc.

Library of Congress Cataloging-in-Publication Data
Symon, Michael
Michael Symon's carnivore / Michael Symon. —1st ed.
  p. cm.
1. Cooking (Meat) I. Title. II. Title: Carnivore
TX749.S96 2012
641.6'6—dc23   2011052363

ISBN 978-0-30795178-6

Printed in China

Book and cover design by Steven Attardo
Cover photographs by Jennifer May

10 9 8 7 6 5 4 3 2 1

First Edition

To Lizzie

CONTENTS

INTRODUCTION

I'm Michael Symon, and I love meat! No, that is not a confession, but rather a proud proclamation. I'm not sure if it's my Midwestern upbringing or my caveman good looks, but as long as I can remember, my favorite meals have always been built around meat. Whether it's been my grandmother's hearty Bolognese—a flavorful sauce of ground beef paired with slightly acidic tomatoes, salty Parmesan, and buttery noodles—or a platter of succulent braised chicken thighs and kale topped with crunchy bread crumbs, meat has always managed to bring a smile to my face.

Meat can play the starring role, as in the case of a show-stopping roast of prime rib, which I think about for special occasions, or it can play the supporting role, as with a mess o' bacon-studded Southern greens, which is more how I eat every day. Regardless, meat always has a way of elevating a dish, a meal, even an entire celebration.

I hope as you read through this book you'll learn not only some great techniques for cooking meat—and how to pick the right one for the right cut of meat, from braising for pork shoulder to pan-frying for chicken livers—but also some appreciation for where it comes from. The source—and rearing—of an animal is as important as any single recipe. Happy animals make better-tasting animals, I swear. Quality never comes cheaply, I know. But if we just trim down our portion sizes, we might discover that a small but intensely flavored dry-aged rib eye is better than a cheap and tasteless chop twice the size. So, first things first: Let's agree to eat less—but *better*—meat.

It is such a crazy time for food in America. On the one hand, we are making tremendous strides in sustainable food, with wonderful farmers' markets springing up all over the place selling fresh, local, wholesome, and compassionately raised foods. It seems easier now than ever to track down good—and I mean "good" in the most humane sense of the word—beef, chicken, lamb, pork, and game. On the other hand, fast-food restaurants continue replicating with alarming speed, bringing with them a rise in obesity, diabetes, and general ill health. Grocery stores are no better, with shelves bulging beneath the weight of processed foods manufactured with ingredients known only to chemists in white lab coats rather than farmers in overalls. While

I would love it if we all bought only local, organic, humanely raised meats, I know that is neither practical nor realistic—even for me. Instead, let's just agree to do a better job when it comes to shopping for, cooking, and consuming meat (see box, page 13).

I also hope to inspire you to cook with not just the popular cuts of popular meats—the beef steaks, pork loins, lamb chops, and chicken breasts—but also meats like rabbit and goat, and the so-called "off cuts" or "fifth quarters," the bits and pieces many home cooks find intimidating (and many diners call *"weird,"* which breaks my heart, no pun intended), from trotters and livers to tripe and sweetbreads. Rather than just living high on the hog, as the saying goes, let's be more adventurous—and resourceful—when it comes to meat cookery. We should all be eating more rabbit: It is such a sustainable meat that takes on other flavors so well. Goat is delightfully gamy. And there is absolutely no reason to waste any good and usable parts of an animal—especially when they happen to be incredibly delicious (and often less expensive)!

Meat is rarely the only item on a plate, platter, or dinner table, and I'd love to shake things up a bit in terms of how we think about its traditional dance partners. Order a chop at a steak house and you'll most likely be served a filet of beef with a side of mashed potatoes and some rich, buttery gravy. Wrong, wrong, *wrong!* First off, filet is the saddest cut of beef on the whole steer, saddled as it is with little flavor and even less texture. Then pairing that limp, insipid filet with baby-food-like mashed spuds is a double whammy: Soft-on-soft texture is never a good thing. And that heavy, fatty sauce concealing the whole affair? I assure you that it does nothing to improve the

taste, texture, or visual interest of the dish.

In my kitchens—both at home and at the "shops"—I strive to counter meat's inherent richness, fattiness, and intenseness (all the things we love about it!) with an equal and appropriate measure of acid, salinity, and texture. This formula is what makes a dish a glorious symphony as opposed to a sad one-note song. Only on occasion will I pair a piece of meat with a rich sauce or a starchy side (unless it's pasta). More likely, the centerpiece of my dishes will be matched with a tart green salad, a spicy pickled vegetable, or a citrusy fruit garnish that will enhance rather than muddy the flavors. Here's an example of perfection in my opinion: a deeply marbled, intensely flavored, slightly charred, grilled dry-aged rib eye paired with a salad of spicy radishes, peppery arugula, and zippy lemon dressing. To help give you some new pairing ideas, I've included some of my favorite sides (and a couple of sauces) to round out your meat dinners.

Whether you're cooking a weeknight meal for the family or pulling out all the stops for a celebratory dinner party, you'll find some great options in these pages. There's the simple but always satisfying Veal Sirloin Minute Steaks—topped with a refreshing Tomato Salad with Red Onion & Dill—that's perfect any night of the week. Or, when the occasion is special and time allows, make the festive and fantastic Pork Pie. In fact, make two, because leftovers are almost as good as the first slice.

Finally, from one meat lover to another: May your steaks always be crusty on the outside and medium-rare in the center, may your potatoes be crispy and duck-fat fried, may you always have bacon in the fridge, and may your side dishes be fresh, seasonal, and brimming with flavor.

CHEW ON THIS

HERE ARE SOME GUIDELINES THAT WE SHOULD ALL STRIVE TO ADHERE TO WHEN IT COMES TO BUYING AND EATING MEAT AND OTHER INGREDIENTS:

» Try to be more aware of where your food comes from and how it's raised. Support your local farmers!

» Avoid as much as possible meats raised with hormones and antibiotics, and produce grown with pesticides, herbicides, and chemical fertilizers.

» Try to eat seasonally, buying foods that are ripe now and—as often as is possible or practical—grown or raised near where you live.

» Try to buy whole, fresh foods as often as possible, and study and understand the ingredients lists when you do purchase prepared or processed foods.

» Know that animal fats are not the devil; hydrogenated fats are.

» Know that so-called diet and low-fat foods are often loaded with sugar, sodium, and chemicals and are actually making Americans fatter!

» Eat fewer—but better—foods.

» Cook and eat with family and friends as often as possible—food always tastes better in good company!

RIB-EYE

PORTERHOUSE

BEEF

PRIME RIB

VEAL
HEART

VEAL
SIRLOINS

TRIPE

POT ROAST

SPLIT VEAL
MARROW BONES

VEAL SHANK
FOR OSSOBUCO

While I personally think that pork is the king of all meats, I know that when most people hear the word "meat," they tend to think of beef. And why not? Who doesn't love a perfectly grilled T-bone or a fork-tender pot roast? And don't get me started on the unparalleled joy of a great burger.

There are so many buzzwords these days at the market that it can be confusing when it comes to buying beef. Organic. Grain-fed. Grass-fed. Pastured. Conventional. Natural. Then there are the myriad cuts. Flank. Porterhouse. Prime rib. Tenderloin. Sirloin. Brisket. Don't forget about the grading. USDA prime. Choice. Select. And what's this about dry-aging versus wet-aging? Is it any wonder shoppers get shell-shocked when they walk into a store trying to figure out what to cook for dinner that night?

After years of buying, cooking, and eating beef, I've figured out which types and cuts of beef work best for certain techniques and recipes. So let's take a trip to the meat section and figure this all out together.

HOW TO CHOOSE BEEF

The value of a great butcher cannot be overestimated. Unfortunately, they can be few and far between. If you are lucky enough to have a local butcher who can walk you through the sometimes confusing beef-shopping process, congratulations. At the very least, a good butcher will know what he or she is selling and how best to cook it. Our Main Meat Man (or Woman) should be able to point out which of his products are grass-fed, grain-fed, or perhaps pasture-raised (read on). Perhaps, too, the butcher may be able to pinpoint the precise source of the beef, down to the very farm on which it was raised. Is the beef USDA prime or choice? The grade will determine how much intramuscular fat the meat has. The best

WIENCEK'S MEATS

beef is well-marbled, streaked with downy white fat lines throughout the muscle. (This is not the same thing as a wide band of fat on the outside of the steak, which does little to improve the beef's flavor and texture.) The more marbling, the higher the grade, and the higher the cost.

In a perfect world, you and your butcher will develop a relationship built upon trust. Ask him or her to allow you to look, touch, and even smell the beef before buying it. Quality beef should be rather dry and only somewhat tacky to the touch; it should not have a very wet exterior. It should still be soft. Examine the color of the beef. It should be deep red—almost bordering on purple. And it should never be suffocated in plastic. Stay away from beef that is bright pink or fire engine red, as it has probably been gassed with carbon monoxide to preserve—unnaturally—its color. A properly aged steak

will hold its deep red color long after it's trimmed.

So, what do you do if you don't have a friendly neighborhood butcher? For starters you can see if any of your local grocery stores has an actual in-house butcher with a handful of common beef sense. Dealing with a real-live person who can answer questions and fill special orders is the next best thing to having a butcher shop. If the only option left is roaming the chilled meat cases stacked with individual plastic-wrapped slabs of beef, there is still hope. Even the largest supermarket chains have begun carrying USDA organic beef—and this should be your first choice. This label guarantees that the beef has eaten only organic vegetable matter, has access to pasture, and has not been administered antibiotics or growth hormones. Also good is "Certified Humane Raised and Handled," which bars antibiotics and growth hormones. Sadly, labels like "all natural" and "natural" don't mean what they sound like as even these animals can be pumped up with nasty stuff.

HOW GRADING WORKS

USDA grading is based on the amount of intramuscular fat—often called "marbling"— that exists within the beef. Following the mantra that says "fat is flavor," beef with more marbling receives a higher grade. Beef with the highest level of intramuscular fat gets labeled Prime, while Choice and Select each contain slightly less respectively. The best beef comes from only steer—male cattle. Beef that comes from old dairy cows is of very low quality and is ground up and used primarily in the fast food business. That's why claims like "100% beef" don't mean much and should be taken with a grain of salt.

GRASS-FED VS. GRAIN-FED

The grass-fed versus grain-fed issue can be confusing even for well-informed shoppers. Americans have been eating grain-fed beef— steer that have been raised on at least some grain—for more than a hundred years. Just because the beef is grain-fed doesn't mean it was conventionally raised in a huge commercial feedlot. There are plenty of humanely raised steer that grow up eating both grass and grain.

Steer that are raised exclusively on grass will typically come from smaller farms, be harder to find, and definitely more expensive than grain-fed. It takes a grass-fed steer much longer to reach market size than its grain-fed equivalent, which explains the high prices. Grass-fed beef is leaner, rich in flavor, and has significantly more omega-3 fatty acids—"good fat"—than grain-fed beef. Grass-fed beef is also gentler on the environment because all that corn requires large amounts of pesticides and fertilizer to grow.

At the end of the day, the decisions should be your own based on what you can spend, what tastes good to you, and what products you can find near you. Personally, I'm not a huge fan of how grass-fed beef tastes. To me, it tastes iron-y. But I do take the time to seek out good-quality grain-fed beef. I just think we all make better decisions when we take the time to get informed.

WHY—AND WHEN—AGING IS IMPORTANT

If you are lucky enough to have access to a butcher who sells USDA Prime beef, he or she likely will have a dry aging room. Aging beef not only intensifies the flavor, it also tenderizes the meat—a win-win, especially for meat that is destined for the grill or a roasting pan. I describe dry-aged beef as tasting slightly musky, but totally delicious. Properly dry-aged beef is pricey, because a lot of the product is lost in the final trimming process. Plus, a lot of the water weight has evaporated. For sure, a USDA Prime dry-aged steak is a pricey but rare treat. If you can't find dry-aged beef locally, you can always order online from a good supplier. Wet-aged beef is another name for beef that has been sealed up in plastic to prevent spoilage. Although time spent in the bag does tenderize the meat, it doesn't do anything for the flavor.

COOK IT RIGHT: BEEF & VEAL
VENISON, ELK, AND OTHER LARGE GAME*

As a general rule, smaller, leaner cuts from these animals work best on the grill, under the broiler, or pan-roasted. Tougher and/or fattier cuts like chucks, shanks, and short ribs benefit from long, moist cooking such as in a braise or stew. When it comes to the oven, think large cuts like rib roasts or special cuts like marrow bones. When preparing sausage and other ground meats, remember that fat is your friend.

GRILL/PAN-ROAST/BROIL

» Porterhouse
» Rib eye or rib chop
» Strip
» Sirloin
» Flank
» Skirt
» Hanger
» Heart
» Sweetbreads
» Kidneys

BRAISE

» Short ribs
» Brisket/breast
» Cheek

» Shank
» Chuck
» Oxtail
» Bottom round
» Tongue

OVEN-ROAST

» Prime rib
» Top round
» Rump
» Marrow
» Saddle

STEW

» Tripe
» Shoulder

SMOKE

» Brisket/breast
» Short ribs
» Cheeks
» Prime rib
» Tongue

GRIND

» Short ribs
» Brisket
» Sirloin
» Chuck

Tenderloin and filet are omitted from this list because I don't like to cook or eat them!

POT ROAST WITH CARROTS, SHALLOTS, MINT & LEMON

On a blustery winter day in Cleveland, nothing gets my family and friends around the kitchen table faster than a flavorful pot roast. This is the ultimate comfort food, and as it slowly simmers away on the stove, intoxicating aromas fill the entire house. I love to serve this dish on a big platter garnished with all the melted carrots and shallots from the pot. I finish it with lemon zest and mint leaves to brighten it up and cut through the roast's rich goodness. Try this dish and I'm sure it will become a cold-weather staple in your home like it has in mine.

1 (5-pound) chuck blade roast, silver skin removed

Kosher salt

1 pound slab bacon, cut into large dice

8 medium carrots, peeled and cut into 2-inch pieces

20 shallots, peeled

5 garlic cloves, smashed and peeled

2 teaspoons coriander seeds

2 bay leaves, fresh or dried

2 cups apple cider

4 (12-ounce) bottles of wheat beer

10 sprigs fresh thyme

About 2 quarts chicken broth, preferably homemade (page 163)

1 cup fresh mint leaves, torn

Grated zest of 2 lemons

1 Season the roast liberally with 2 tablespoons salt and refrigerate overnight.

2 An hour before cooking, remove the roast from the fridge.

3 Preheat the oven to 350°F.

4 In a large Dutch oven, cook the bacon over medium heat until slightly crispy. Remove the bacon and set aside, leaving the drippings in the pan. Dry the roast with a paper towel and begin to brown it in the bacon fat for 2 minutes per side. When browned on all sides, remove the meat and set aside.

5 Add to the pot the carrots, shallots, garlic, and a pinch of salt and cook until the vegetables begin to caramelize, about 4 minutes. Add the coriander and bay leaves and cook for another minute. Deglaze the pot with the apple cider, scraping up the browned bits on the bottom of the pot with a wooden spoon. This gives the dish more depth and richness. Add the beer and thyme and bring to a simmer.

6 Return the roast to the pot along with the cooked bacon and enough broth to cover the meat. The braising liquid will reduce considerably while in the oven. Cover the pot and put in the oven. Cook until the meat is tender, 3 to 4 hours, basting every hour. Remove from the oven and skim off the excess fat.

7 Carefully move the roast to a large platter. Spoon the vegetables and sauce on top, discard the bay leaves and thyme, and garnish with the mint and lemon zest.

VEAL SIRLOIN MINUTE STEAKS

Minute steaks are a great way to get a quick, affordable meal on the table. Ask your butcher to pound veal (or beef) top sirloin into thin steaks, or do it yourself. Because these steaks are pan-fried, they develop a caramelized crust with intense flavor. If you fry these steaks in bacon fat, like I do, you'll end up with an even tastier dish. In the middle of summer, when tomatoes are at their best, I top these steaks with Tomato Salad with Red Onion & Dill (page 207). The refreshing coolness of the salad is the perfect balance to the spicy steaks.

4 (4-ounce) veal sirloin steaks

Kosher salt

All-purpose flour, for dredging

2 tablespoons bacon fat

2 garlic cloves, unpeeled, smashed

2 Thai chiles, split lengthwise

1 Lay out the steaks on a cutting board and cover them with a large piece of plastic wrap. With a meat mallet, pound the steaks to ¼-inch thickness.

2 Season the steaks with salt and dredge them with flour, shaking off any excess. Heat a large cast-iron skillet over medium-high heat. When the pan is hot, add the bacon fat, garlic, and chiles. Add the steaks to the pan and cook for 1 minute per side until browned. Before removing the steaks from the pan, swirl them around with the aromatics to pick up some of that great flavor.

3 Remove the steaks from the pan and discard the garlic and chiles. Serve immediately.

GRILLED RIB EYES WITH WATERCRESS, BLUE CHEESE & RADISH SALAD

Rib eye is my absolute favorite cut of beef: It's fatty, tender, and delicious. At my restaurants, we age USDA prime rib eyes for 24 to 30 days. The process results in an incredibly juicy, flavorful steak. These chops are best grilled over lump charcoal, as nothing compares to the taste that comes from cooking over live fire. If you don't have access to a live-fire grill, a powerful gas grill will do. I like to pair grilled rib eye with a crisp watercress and radish salad to cut through the fatty richness. And what goes better with beef than some good, earthy blue cheese?

4 (1-pound) beef rib-eye steaks, preferably dry-aged USDA prime

Kosher salt and freshly ground black pepper

½ cup champagne vinegar

3 tablespoons minced shallot

2 tablespoons honey

2 tablespoons Dijon mustard

¾ cup extra-virgin olive oil

2 cups sliced radishes

4 cups watercress

2 cups crumbled blue cheese, preferably Wisconsin

1 Heat a charcoal or gas grill to medium-high.

2 Season the steaks with salt and pepper. Grill the steaks to the desired doneness, 3 to 5 minutes per side for medium-rare. Remove from the grill and let rest, uncovered, for 10 minutes.

3 Meanwhile, in a medium bowl, combine the vinegar, shallot, honey, Dijon mustard, and ½ teaspoon salt. Slowly whisk in the olive oil. Add the radishes and watercress to the dressing and toss to combine. Sprinkle the blue cheese over the top.

4 To serve, divide the watercress salad and the steaks among 4 plates.

PAN-ROASTED SIRLOIN WITH CHANTERELLES & SOY

This is one of those dishes that appears on the plate to be so much more complicated than it really is. The truth is, it's super easy to prepare and you *still* end up looking like a kitchen rock star. If you happen to be a fan of filet mignon, give top sirloin a try. It's just like beef tenderloin, only with twice the flavor for half the price. Talk about win-win!

1 (2-pound) top sirloin steak

Kosher salt

½ teaspoon sugar

2 tablespoons plus
1 tablespoon canola oil

1 pound chanterelle
mushrooms, cleaned
and sliced

1 shallot, sliced

2 garlic cloves, minced

1 tablespoon fresh
thyme leaves

½ cup dry red wine

1 tablespoon
soy sauce

1 tablespoon
grainy mustard

1 tablespoon
unsalted butter

1 Season the sirloin with 2 teaspoons salt and the sugar, cover, and refrigerate overnight.

2 Remove the sirloin from the fridge and allow to come to room temperature before cooking, about 30 minutes.

3 Heat the 2 tablespoons oil in a large roasting pan over medium-high heat. Pat the steak dry with a paper towel, put it in the pan, and cook for 3 to 4 minutes per side, or until browned, for medium rare. If you prefer your steak cooked past medium-rare, cook for an additional minute per side. Move the steak to a plate to rest.

4 To the same pan over medium-high heat, add the 1 tablespoon oil. Add the mushrooms with a pinch of salt and cook, turning once, for 4 minutes, or until caramelized. Reduce the heat to medium, add the shallot, and cook for 1 minute. Add the garlic and cook for 1 minute. Pour off any excess fat in the pan, add the thyme, and cook for another minute, or until the thyme releases its aroma. Add the wine and let it simmer and reduce by half while scraping up the browned bits from the pan with a wooden spoon. Add the soy sauce, mustard, and butter and whisk until the butter is melted and fully incorporated. Remove from the heat and add any juices that accumulated from the plate with the resting sirloin.

5 To serve, thinly slice the sirloin against the grain, put it on a platter, and spoon the mushroom sauce over the top.

ROASTING

There are two basic methods of roasting: pan and oven. Pan-roasting is great for smaller cuts of meat, while oven-roasting works better for the big ones. For pan-roasting, as with braising (see page 201), it's key to get the pan and fat good and hot, use dry, room-temperature meat, not crowd the pan, and *leave the meat alone* until it develops a great crust and releases from the pan. When both sides are well seared, add some butter and any herbs or aromatics you're using to the pan. Use a spoon to baste the meat several times before placing the pan in the oven to finish. The oven should not be set higher than 325°F. Every now and then, open the oven and baste the meat. When the meat reaches your desired doneness, pull the pan from the oven, baste the meat, and let it rest for at least 10 minutes before serving.

With oven-roasting, the whole process is done in the oven. The oven is set higher—375°F or more—to sear the meat. Then it's reduced to 325°F or lower, which gives the fat in larger cuts plenty of time to melt, producing a juicier, more tender dish. Instead of occasional bastings, I cover the meat with a piece of cheesecloth dipped in herb-infused butter. This self-basting system means the oven door stays shut and the meat is done sooner. When the meat is done, remove the cheesecloth and let the meat rest for a minimum of 3 minutes per pound.

PRIME RIB

Serves 6

Prime rib is one of the most expensive cuts on the entire beast—and for good reason! It has every-thing you could want in a cut of beef. The bones and fat add tons of flavor, and when cooked properly, the meat is melt-in-your-mouth tender. While I love a great rare steak, prime rib actually benefits from a little more cooking. Taking this to medium-rare (or a shade past) allows the fat to melt and baste the meat while pulling more flavor from the bones. When ordering prime rib from your butcher, request the loin end. Also, ask that he or she take the meat off the ribs. But don't leave the bones behind—you'll use them as the roasting rack! Since the beef is wonderful on its own, I limit the garnishes to some zippy horseradish beets and peppery arugula. It is crucial to take the meat out of the fridge an hour before cooking and to let the roast rest for at least 20 minutes before slicing it. Otherwise, all the yummy juices will be left on the cutting board!

1 (4-bone) prime rib, bones and excess fat removed and reserved

4 teaspoons kosher salt

Freshly ground black pepper

4 sprigs fresh rosemary

4 garlic cloves, unpeeled, smashed

4 ounces arugula

2 teaspoons extra-virgin olive oil

2 cups Horseradish Beets (page 233)

1 Liberally season the prime rib with the salt and some pepper and refrigerate overnight.

2 An hour before cooking, remove the roast from the refrigerator to allow it to come to room temperature.

3 Meanwhile, preheat the oven to 400°F.

4 Put the reserved ribs in a roasting pan bowed-side-up. Scatter any fat and meat trimmings in the pan around the bones. Roast the bones and trimmings for about 30 minutes, or until the fat starts to render.

5 Remove the pan from the oven, put the rosemary sprigs on top of the bones, and then top with the prime rib. The ribs will be acting as the roasting rack. Put the smashed garlic in the bottom of the pan with the trimmings. Baste the beef with the fat drippings and return the pan to the oven.

6 Cook for 30 minutes and then baste the roast again.

7 Reduce the heat to 350°F and cook until the meat is medium-rare (an internal temperature of 125° to 130°F), about 1 hour and 15 minutes. Keep basting the roast every 30 minutes until it is done. Keep in mind that the roast will continue to cook while resting.

8 Remove the roast from the oven and put it on a cutting board to rest, uncovered, for 20 minutes. Slice the prime rib to the desired thickness and garnish with the arugula, olive oil, and horseradish beets.

BROILED PORTERHOUSE

In most steak houses, the steaks and chops are cooked under high-powered broilers. But for some reason, it is a method few home cooks feel comfortable using. In fact, when I suggest broiling steaks at home to people, they look at me like I'm crazy. Let me assure you that, other than the nuisance of a little bit of smoke, there is no easier way to cook a steak. (Just open a window or two before starting.) Better still, your friends will be impressed that you can broil something other than garlic bread.

2 (24-ounce) dry-aged USDA prime porterhouse steaks

Kosher salt

4 strips bacon

Roasted Garlic with Parsley & Lemon (page 243)

1 Liberally season the steaks on both sides with kosher salt, using about 1 teaspoon per steak. Refrigerate overnight.

2 Remove the steaks from the fridge 45 minutes before cooking to let them come to room temperature.

3 Arrange a rack 8 inches from the top heat source and preheat the broiler to its highest setting.

4 Arrange the bacon in a large cast-iron grill pan and set the pan on the top rack under the broiler. When the bacon is crispy (about 3 minutes per side), remove it from the pan to a paper towel. When cool enough to handle, crumble it and set aside.

5 Put the steaks in the same pan and broil for 4 minutes. Carefully flip the steaks and broil for another 4 minutes. At this point, the steaks should be medium-rare. (If you prefer them medium, cook for about 6 minutes per side.)

6 Remove the steaks from the broiler, schmear with roasted garlic, and top with the crumbled bacon. Let the steaks rest, uncovered, for 5 minutes, before slicing and serving.

KILLER HOT DOGS

Nothing evokes memories of childhood quite like a hot dog. Regardless of whether I was at a Cleveland Indians game with my dad, attending a big family picnic, or going to a neighborhood cookout down the block, I always made a beeline for the hot dogs. There are lots of great hot dogs that you can purchase with "snappy" natural casings and good beefy flavor. But if you're feeling a little adventurous and want to give making your own dogs a shot, this is my favorite recipe.

1 pound beef suet

1 pound beef chuck roast, fat and sinew removed, cut into large dice

2½ tablespoons kosher salt

½ teaspoon pink curing salt

1¼ cups 2% milk, frozen into ice cubes

2 tablespoons raw sugar

1 teaspoon dextrose powder

1 teaspoon garlic powder

1½ tablespoons Colman's mustard powder

1 teaspoon smoked paprika

1 teaspoon Hungarian hot paprika

1 teaspoon chipotle powder

1 teaspoon ground coriander

¼ teaspoon ground nutmeg

¼ teaspoon ground white pepper

5 feet of hog casing, soaked overnight

1 In order to achieve the proper texture and emulsion in the hot dogs, it is important to chill all the sausage-making equipment beforehand. This includes the grinding attachments, blade and dies, and sausage-casing bowl, plus the mixing bowl and paddle attachment for the mixer. To chill the equipment, simply put it in the freezer or submerge it in an ice bath until very cold.

2 Combine the beef suet with ¼ cup water in a heavy-bottomed saucepan. Set over very low heat for several hours until completely rendered. Do not let the fat come to a boil or brown, as it will taste harsh. When the suet is completely liquefied, strain through a very-fine-mesh sieve or a piece of cheesecloth. Let the strained liquid cool in the refrigerator. When chilled and solid, cut into large dice and reserve. You will only use 10 ounces (about 1¼ cups) of the fat.

3 Put the diced beef and the 10 ounces diced suet in the freezer until very cold. Pass each through the large grinding die onto a baking sheet, keeping the beef separate from the fat. Return both to the freezer until they are crunchy, but not frozen solid, about 20 minutes.

4 Combine the meat and fat with the kosher salt, pink curing salt, and milk ice cubes. Grind all of this through the small die into the chilled mixing bowl. Add the rest of the seasonings and mix with the chilled paddle attachment on high for 8 minutes. To keep things cool, it might be necessary to hold 2-quart freezer bags filled with ice on the outside of the bowl while mixing. After 8 minutes, the mixture should resemble a very stiff batter that is slightly tacky. Keep refrigerated until ready to use.

5 Open one end of the hog casing and put it onto the kitchen faucet (like you're filling a water balloon). Run water through the inside of the casing until it comes out the other end. Repeat this process. Rinsing the casing twice not only cleans it thoroughly, but also stretches it out a bit, making it

(RECIPE CONTINUES)

easier to thread onto the sausage-stuffer tube. Keep the casing submerged in water until ready to use.

6 Set up your sausage stuffer according to the manufacturer's instructions. Stuff the mixture into the casing and twist into 6-inch links. Refrigerate, uncovered, overnight or for up to 3 days. For a hot dog with more "snap," go the whole 3 days.

7 Poach the hot dogs in 170°F water until they reach an internal temperature of 140°F. This takes about 20 minutes. Transfer to an ice bath to chill thoroughly. Remove from the ice bath, pat dry, and cut between the hot dogs to separate them. Grill until marked and heated through before serving.

GRINDING

There are many benefits to grinding your own meat, not the least of which is saving cash. One of the most compelling reasons, though, is that you control the quality of what goes into the mix. Working with whole pieces of meat makes the final sausage or burger safer to eat at temperatures less than well-done, as there is less of a chance of bacteria. Grinding meat at home also gives you total control over the fat-to-meat ratio. For optimum flavor and texture, I recommend 20 to 25 percent fat for burgers and 30 percent fat for sausages. Before weighing out the meat and the fat, be sure to remove all sinew and silver skin. For the best flavor, I like to season the meat 8 to 24 hours before grinding to allow the salt and spices to penetrate the meat. This technique enhances both flavor and texture. When grinding meat, make sure all the equipment is well chilled—the meat, the grinder, all mixing bowls and spoons—to make the process go as smoothly as possible. Warm fat is a bear to grind. I like to have the meat in a bowl sitting in a larger bowl of ice.

DOUBLE-TROUBLE MEAT LOAF

Whenever I think of meat loaf, I think of the scene in *A Christmas Story* (filmed in Cleveland—woo-hoo!) when Randy—who is dreading his mother's meat loaf—says, "Meatloaf, smeatloaf, double-beatloaf. I hate meatloaf." Man, that movie just slays me. While I have no idea what was in Mrs. Parker's meat loaf, I can bet this version will make you and your children much, much happier.

Nonstick cooking spray

2 tablespoons unsalted butter

1 medium yellow onion, minced

Kosher salt

2 garlic cloves, minced

1 teaspoon smoked paprika

1 teaspoon chipotle powder

2 cups small-diced day-old bread (crust removed)

½ cup whole milk

1½ pounds ground chuck

8 ounces ground bacon

2 large eggs

2 tablespoons finely chopped fresh flat-leaf parsley

Freshly ground black pepper

1 Preheat the oven to 350°F. Spray a 4 by 10-inch loaf pan with nonstick cooking spray.

2 In a medium sauté pan over medium heat, combine the butter, onion, and ¼ teaspoon salt. Cook for 1 to 2 minutes, until the onion is softened. Add the garlic and cook for 1 minute. Add the paprika and chipotle powder and cook for 1 minute to lightly toast the spices. Remove the mixture from the heat and set aside to cool.

3 Meanwhile, in a medium bowl, soak the bread in the milk. After the bread has thoroughly absorbed the milk, remove it from the bowl, squeezing out any excess liquid.

4 Transfer the bread to a large bowl and add the onion mixture, ground chuck, ground bacon, eggs, and parsley. Season with pepper and mix to thoroughly combine. Pack into the prepared loaf pan, place on a baking sheet, and bake for 1 hour, or until a thermometer inserted into the center registers 160°F. Remove from the oven and let cool slightly, which makes it easier to slice.

5 Unmold the meat loaf, slice, and serve. Refrigerate leftovers for a great cold sandwich or late-night snack!

BEEF JERKY

Making jerky is a lost art. It was something people did hundreds of years ago before refrigeration to preserve meat following the hunt. When I would go to the West Side Market with my Pap as a kid, our first stop was always to grab some jerky. Our intention was to have some to bring home, but we usually ended up eating it all before we even left. Back then, I didn't care where my jerky came from so long as it was chewy, salty, and a little spicy. But as I grew older, I became obsessed with finding the perfect jerky. Ironically, the best I ever found was at the West Side Market all along, at the J & J Meats stand. This recipe is my attempt to re-create that perfect jerky, which was not too heavily spiced, allowing the natural beef flavor to really shine.

2 pounds eye of round, trimmed of all fat

1½ tablespoons kosher salt

2 teaspoons sugar

2 teaspoons garlic powder

1 teaspoon onion powder

1 teaspoon cayenne pepper

1 teaspoon chipotle powder

½ teaspoon ground coriander

½ teaspoon smoked paprika

1 Slice the beef with the grain into strips about 1 inch thick by 3 inches long. If the strips appear too large, they likely are the correct size, as they will shrink significantly during the cooking process.

2 In a mixing bowl, mix the remaining ingredients. Liberally season the beef with this spice mixture, being sure to use it all. Cover the beef and refrigerate for 24 hours.

3 Preheat the oven to 250°F.

4 Put the strips on a baking-rack-lined sheet pan. Arrange the meat so that the strips are not touching or overlapping. This allows for even drying. Bake for 6 to 7 hours, until fairly dry. If you prefer your jerky on the chewy side, remove it after 6 hours. Otherwise, leave it in for the full 7 hours to dry it out some more.

5 Stored in an airtight container at room temperature, beef jerky will last for several months.

NITRITE-FREE CORNED BEEF

In Cleveland, corned beef is king and is served at nearly every corner deli in town. There's nothing like the mile-high sandwiches dished up at Slyman's, where buttery folds of rosy beef are stacked on soft rye bread. This recipe is my take on this rightly famous sandwich. Although the meat will taste just as good as the original, it won't be pink, because this version is made without nitrites.

2 pounds kosher salt

1 pound packed light brown sugar

4 bay leaves, fresh or dried

3 tablespoons black peppercorns

2 tablespoons crushed juniper berries

1 tablespoon crushed coriander seeds

1 (5-pound) beef brisket

1 medium red onion, peeled and quartered

1 head garlic, halved crosswise

3 medium carrots, peeled and cut into 2-inch pieces

1 bunch celery, cut into 2-inch pieces

1 (750 ml) bottle white wine

1 In a nonreactive pot, combine 6 quarts water, the salt, brown sugar, bay leaves, peppercorns, juniper berries, and coriander and bring to a simmer, whisking until the salt and sugar are dissolved. Chill this mixture completely. Put the brisket in a deep container large enough to accommodate it. Pour the chilled liquid over the meat, weighting the brisket down with a plate to keep it fully submerged. Allow to marinate in the refrigerator for 4 days.

2 Remove the brisket from the corning liquid, rinse it, and pat dry with paper towels. Discard the corning liquid.

3 In a large stockpot, combine the onion, garlic, carrots, celery, and wine. Add enough water to cover the brisket and bring to a simmer. Add the brisket and simmer for 3 hours, or until the meat is fork-tender. Carefully remove the brisket from the cooking liquid and let it cool slightly. (If desired, cool completely, cover, and refrigerate for up to 1 week. Reheat before serving.) Thinly slice it across the grain before serving.

CURING

I am a huge fan of curing meats, whether it's a quick cure for anything heading for the grill, oven, or stovetop, or the long cures that transform various cuts of meat into items like prosciutto and coppa. While not many home cooks will venture into the art and science of the long cure, all should embrace the quick cure. Simply by seasoning meat well in advance of cooking—between 8 and 24 hours—we can greatly enhance the flavor and texture of the final dish. The added time gives the salt and other spices time to penetrate the meat, which produces a more consistent seasoning. The salt also helps the cells in the protein retain moisture, producing a juicier piece of meat when cooked. More flavor. Juicier texture. Little effort. Who wouldn't want that?!

CORNED BEEF HASH

When making corned beef sandwiches, you will always have lots of leftover trimmings. What better way to use them up than in my all-time-favorite breakfast: corned beef hash? This recipe definitely isn't the classic hash, but it is my preferred version. The addition of caramelized onion and jalapeño gives it a touch of sweetness along with a good old-fashioned kick of heat. I think the sweet heat is the perfect complement to balance the salty corned beef and starchy potatoes. This recipe is great presented on a big platter topped with your favorite style of eggs. My vote is for fried!

8 ounces fingerling potatoes

Kosher salt

1 tablespoon unsalted butter

1 medium yellow onion, cut into medium dice

1 jalapeño, seeded and minced

1 garlic clove, minced

8 ounces corned beef, homemade (see opposite) or store-bought, shredded

Freshly ground black pepper

3 tablespoons thinly sliced fresh cilantro leaves

1 Put the potatoes in a large pot, add cold water to cover by an inch, and season generously with salt. Bring to a boil over medium-high heat. Cook the potatoes until al dente, about 10 minutes. Remove from the water and let cool. When the potatoes have cooled, cut them into medium dice.

2 In a 12-inch sauté pan over medium-high heat, combine the butter, onion, and a pinch of salt. Cook for 4 to 5 minutes, until translucent. Add the jalapeño and garlic and cook for 1 minute. Raise the heat to high and add the potatoes. Cook the potatoes until golden brown, tossing occasionally, about 8 to 10 minutes, and then add the corned beef. Cook for 2 to 3 minutes, until the corned beef is heated through.

3 Taste the hash and add salt and pepper as needed. Remove from the heat, stir in the cilantro, and serve.

PASTRAMI

Pastrami is like the bacon of beef: It's smoky, fatty, flavorful, and aggressively seasoned. While great on its own, pastrami can also be used to send dishes over the top, like with the popular Fat Doug Burger (page 44) at my B Spot burger restaurant. I also love to use pastrami in place of corned beef in hash or to liven up a pan of roasted potatoes. Just think of pastrami like bacon's beefy bro and the possibilities become infinite.

1½ cups kosher salt

½ cup granulated sugar

8 teaspoons pink curing salt

1 tablespoon Pickling Spice (recipe follows)

½ cup packed dark brown sugar

½ cup honey

2 tablespoons minced garlic

1 (5-pound) beef brisket, surface fat removed

1 tablespoon coriander seeds, toasted and ground

1 tablespoon black peppercorns, toasted and ground

1 In a nonreactive saucepan, combine 1 gallon water with the kosher salt, granulated sugar, pink curing salt, pickling spice, brown sugar, honey, and garlic and bring to a simmer, whisking until the salts and sugars are dissolved. Chill this mixture completely. Put the brisket in a deep container large enough to accommodate it. Pour the chilled brine over the meat, weighting the brisket down with a plate to keep it fully submerged. Allow to marinate in the refrigerator for 3 days.

2 Remove the brisket from the brining liquid, rinse it thoroughly, and pat dry with paper towels. Discard the brine. Blend together the coriander and pepper and coat the brisket with the mixture.

3 Prepare and set a smoker to 200°F. Using apple-wood chips, smoke the brisket until the internal temperature reaches 150°F, about 3 hours. Put the smoked brisket in a roasting pan with 1 inch of water and cover. Return to the smoker and cook at 275°F for another 2 to 3 hours, until fork-tender.

PICKLING SPICE *Makes ¼ cup*

1 tablespoon black peppercorns

1 tablespoon mustard seeds

1 tablespoon coriander seeds

1½ teaspoons red pepper flakes

1½ teaspoons whole allspice

1½ teaspoons ground mace

1½ teaspoons whole cloves

1½ teaspoons ground ginger

1 small cinnamon stick, crushed

10 bay leaves, broken up

Mix together all of the ingredients in a lidded container and store in a cool, dry place for up to 6 months.

FAT DOUG BURGER

This is the burger that made B Spot famous! I named it after my partner, Doug Petkovic, who ironically is quite svelte. But who the heck would order a Skinny Doug? This was our first "meat-on-meat" style hamburger, a concept that proves that everything is better topped with meat—even meat! Turns out we aren't the only ones who think so, as the burger took top honors at the South Beach Wine and Food Festival's Burger Bash. Once you try this pastrami-topped burger, we think you'll agree, too. But don't stop there. Let your imagination go wild and you'll see that there isn't a meat that doesn't go great on a burger!

8 ounces ground sirloin

8 ounces ground brisket

8 ounces ground boneless short rib

Salt and freshly ground black pepper

8 ounces pastrami, thinly sliced

4 slices Swiss cheese

4 brioche or egg buns, split

1½ tablespoons unsalted butter, melted

Coleslaw (page 213)

1 Heat a charcoal or gas grill to medium-high.

2 Mix together the ground sirloin, brisket, and short rib. Form 4 patties of roughly equal size, each about ½ to ¾ inch thick. Season with salt and pepper. Grill the patties until medium-rare, 3 to 5 minutes per side.

3 Divide the pastrami into 4 equal piles. In a sauté pan over medium heat, add the pastrami piles and heat for 2 minutes. Top each pile with a slice of Swiss cheese. When the cheese has melted, after a minute or two, remove the pastrami piles from the pan and set aside.

4 Brush the cut sides of the buns with the butter and toast on the grill for about 2 minutes.

5 To serve, put a burger on the bottom half of each bun, followed by a pastrami pile with cheese, a few tablespoons of coleslaw, and the top bun.

GRILLED VEAL HEARTS

For whatever reason, heart freaks some people out. But it shouldn't; it is just another muscle in the steer—and one that packs a ton of flavor. The truth is, cooked properly, heart eats like a fantastic steak for a third of the price. To prevent this cut of meat from becoming tough and dry, it's crucial not to cook it past medium-rare. So, what are you waiting for? Be adventurous and have a heart.

3 pounds veal hearts, trimmed and cleaned

2 garlic cloves, smashed and peeled

1 teaspoon coriander seeds, toasted

1 teaspoon cracked black peppercorns

2 teaspoons red wine vinegar

1 tablespoon kosher salt

1 sprig fresh rosemary

¾ cup extra-virgin olive oil

Giardiniera (page 225)

1 Put all of the ingredients except the *giardiniera* in a large zip-top bag and shake to coat the hearts. Marinate in the refrigerator overnight or for up to 2 days.

2 About 30 minutes before grilling, remove the hearts from the bag and discard the marinade. Scrape off any bits of coriander and peppercorns that cling to the meat.

3 Meanwhile, heat a charcoal or gas grill to medium-high.

4 Grill the hearts for 2 to 3 minutes per side, until they reach an internal temperature of 120°F. Remove from the grill and let rest for 5 minutes.

5 Slice very thinly against the grain, top with *giardiniera,* and serve.

BEEF TARTARE WITH AVOCADO & UNI MOUSSE

This is a dish I used to great effect on *Iron Chef America:* "Battle Uni." This recipe replaces the capers that customarily appear in the classic version of steak tartare with uni, or sea urchin. As with capers, the uni lends a briny balance to the rich beef. This version of beef tartare was such a hit with the judges on the show that it now makes regular appearances on the menus of my restaurants Roast and Lola. You certainly can omit the uni, but if you have access to it, go ahead and give it a try. This is tartare taken to a whole new level.

AVOCADO & UNI MOUSSE

2 ripe Hass avocados

Grated zest of 1 lemon

2 teaspoons fresh lemon juice

2 teaspoons fresh lime juice

¾ teaspoon kosher salt

3 tablespoons uni (optional)

½ cup heavy cream

BEEF TARTARE

2½ tablespoons grated fresh horseradish

1 large shallot, minced

1½ tablespoons finely chopped fresh flat-leaf parsley

1½ tablespoons capers, finely chopped (omit if using uni)

2 tablespoons Dijon mustard

Grated zest of 1 lemon

1 large egg yolk

1 teaspoon Worcestershire sauce

1 teaspoon kosher salt

¼ teaspoon freshly ground black pepper

1 pound Angus sirloin

TOASTS

1 baguette, sliced into ¼-inch-thick rounds

Extra-virgin olive oil, for brushing

Kosher salt and freshly ground black pepper

1 For the avocado and uni mousse, cut each avocado in half, remove the pit, and scoop the flesh into the bowl of a food processor. Add the lemon zest, lemon juice, lime juice, and salt and puree until smooth. Transfer to a medium mixing bowl. If using the uni, push it through a fine-mesh sieve into the bowl and mix into the avocados.

2 Whip the heavy cream until it holds soft peaks and then gently fold it into the avocado puree. Refrigerate while you prepare the tartare.

3 For the tartare, combine everything but the beef in a medium mixing bowl. Remove all visible fat from the beef and finely dice the meat by hand. For the best texture and appearance, the goal is to end up with small dice as opposed to fine mince. A very sharp chef knife is essential. When diced, fold the beef into the other ingredients, cover, and refrigerate until ready to serve or for up to 30 minutes.

4 For the toasts, preheat the oven to 350°F.

5 Arrange the sliced baguette on a baking sheet, brush with olive oil, and season with salt and pepper. Toast in the oven for about 8 minutes, or until golden brown and crisp. Remove from the oven and set aside to cool.

6 To serve, spoon the tartare onto serving plates and top with the avocado and uni mousse. Arrange the toasts around the tartare.

ROASTED BONE MARROW WITH PARSLEY SALAD

For as long as I can remember, I have always loved roasted bone marrow. At a fund-raising dinner at Lola a few years back, the lovely and talented chef Michelle Bernstein served roasted marrow bones that were split lengthwise. Because I had only ever seen them served upright and whole, it was a revelation! Not only does the fat caramelize better, but the bones are easier and less intimidating to eat. Naturally, I asked Michelle if I could "borrow" her idea and she was kind enough to consent. Marrow is best eaten hot, straight out of the oven. Spoon some onto a piece of grilled bread, top with parsley salad, and enjoy.

3 marrow bones (veal femur bones), split in half lengthwise

1 small baguette

½ teaspoon extra-virgin olive oil, plus more for the bread

¾ cup loosely packed fresh flat-leaf parsley

3 tablespoons Pickled Shallots (page 222)

Juice of ½ lemon

¼ teaspoon flaky sea salt, such as Cyprus Flake or Maldon

1 Submerge the marrow bones in ice water and soak overnight in the refrigerator. This draws out any remaining blood. The marrow will turn from pink to white.

2 Preheat the oven to 375°F.

3 Remove the bones from the water and pat dry. Discard the water. Arrange the bones marrow-side-up on a baking sheet and roast for about 7 minutes, until the marrow becomes very soft and pudding-like.

4 Meanwhile, slice the baguette on the diagonal into ½-inch-thick rounds. Brush each side with olive oil, put on a baking sheet, and toast in the oven for about 5 minutes, or until golden brown. Set aside to cool.

5 Mix together the parsley, pickled shallots, lemon juice, the ½ teaspoon olive oil, and the flaky sea salt.

6 To serve, put the hot roasted marrow bones on a platter, top with the parsley salad, and arrange the grilled bread slices on the side.

STUFFED BRISKET WITH BRAISED CABBAGE

This is a turbo "man meal" at its absolute finest, the kind of dish that will impress your friends, while feeding a small army. Don't let the prep and cooking time scare you away, as the difficulty level is pretty low and the results are gloriously delicious. To trim some time and trouble, ask your butcher to butterfly the brisket for you at the market. You are looking for a 10-inch square that's ¾ to 1 inch thick.

1½ pounds brisket, butterflied and lightly pounded

Kosher salt

4 ounces kale, tough center ribs removed

Freshly ground black pepper

½ large carrot, peeled and cut into matchsticks

½ large parsnip, peeled and cut into matchsticks

8 ounces kielbasa, cut into matchsticks

2 tablespoons canola oil

1 pound slab bacon, cut into thin strips

2 Spanish onions, minced

3 garlic cloves, minced

1 teaspoon red pepper flakes

2 pounds (1 large head) white cabbage, thinly sliced

4 (12-ounce) bottles of stout beer

2 bay leaves, fresh or dried

¼ cup grainy mustard

½ cup chopped fresh flat-leaf parsley

1 Season the brisket with salt. Cover and refrigerate overnight.

2 Bring a large stockpot of water to a rolling boil. Add salt until the water tastes seasoned. Have ready a bowl of ice water. In small batches, blanch the kale leaves in the boiling water for just 10 seconds. Use a slotted spoon to move the kale from the boiling water to the ice bath to stop the cooking. Drain the kale, squeezing it to remove as much water as possible.

3 Preheat the oven to 350°F.

4 Season the meat on both sides with black pepper. Arrange a layer of kale over the entire brisket, being sure to leave a ½-inch border on all sides. Arrange the carrot, parsnip, and kielbasa in a line down the center of the brisket. Roll the meat as tightly as you can, tying it off with kitchen twine in 5 places to secure it.

5 Put a 6-quart Dutch oven over medium-high heat. Add the canola oil and when the oil is hot, sear the brisket on all sides, about 5 minutes per side. When browned, remove the brisket to a plate. Discard any oil left in the pot.

6 In the same pot, cook the bacon over medium heat until it begins to release a good amount of fat and starts to get crispy. Add the onions and cook for 2 to 3 minutes, until they start to get translucent. Add the garlic and red pepper flakes and cook for another minute. Add the cabbage and a pinch of salt. When the cabbage wilts slightly, after a couple of minutes, add the beer and bay leaves and bring to a simmer.

7 Return the meat to the pot, burying it under the cabbage. Cover the pot and transfer to the oven for 1 hour. Flip the roast, bury it under the cabbage again, recover the pot, and cook for another hour or longer, until the meat is fork-tender. Remove the brisket from the pot and put it on a cutting board to rest and let cool slightly. This will make it easier to handle and slice.

8 Meanwhile, whisk the mustard into the braised cabbage mixture. Taste and adjust the seasonings if necessary. Remove the bay leaves.

9 Remove the kitchen twine from the brisket using scissors or a sharp knife. Carefully slice the brisket into ½-inch pieces and arrange on a platter. Spoon the cabbage around the roast and garnish with the chopped parsley.

STEWING

Many home cooks mistakenly believe that stewing and braising are the same technique. That's understandable as both methods transform tough cuts of meats into fork-tender morsels through slow cooking in liquid. But that's where the similarities end. The first major difference is that stews are usually made with smaller, often bite-size pieces of meat. Braising, on the other hand, often involves larger cuts of meat, sometimes still on the bone. Also, stewing is usually prepared from start to finish on the stovetop while braises start on the stove but get finished in a low oven. Perhaps the biggest difference between the two methods is the amount of liquid used. In a braise, the meat isn't submerged in the liquid, which allows the top of it to brown. In a stew, the meat is completely immersed in liquid and allowed to simmer uncovered in the pot until tender. Braises get basted throughout the process; stews are stirred.

BRAISED VEAL SHORT RIBS

Serves
8 to 10

I'm not sure why, but for some reason, beef is the reigning champion when it comes to short ribs. That's fine with me because it makes veal short ribs all the more affordable. I love preparing this great version during the cooler months—and we have a few of those in Cleveland! The richness of the braised meat warms the soul, while the brightness of the gremolata perks up the whole dish. As with all braises, don't forget to baste the meat like a madman/madwoman!

MARINADE

2 cups large-diced celery

2 cups large-diced peeled carrots

2½ cups large-diced red onions

1 Fresno chile, quartered

3 garlic cloves, smashed and peeled

12 sprigs fresh thyme

2 sprigs fresh rosemary

2 bay leaves, fresh or dried

1 tablespoon black peppercorns

1 tablespoon coriander seeds

4 (750 ml) bottles dry red wine

RIBS

10 pounds meaty veal short ribs on the bone

4 tablespoons olive oil

Kosher salt and freshly ground black pepper

All-purpose flour, for dredging

¼ cup tomato paste

2 quarts chicken broth, preferably homemade (page 163)

Flaky sea salt, such as Cyprus Flake or Maldon

Gremolata (page 228)

1 Begin by combining all the marinade ingredients in a container large enough to hold the meat. Submerge the short ribs in the marinade and refrigerate overnight. The next day, remove the ribs from the marinade and pat dry. Strain the aromatics out of the liquid, reserving both the wine and the aromatics separately.

2 Heat 2 tablespoons of the olive oil in a large enameled Dutch oven over medium-high heat. Season the short ribs with kosher salt and pepper and then dredge with flour, making sure to pat off any excess.

3 Brown the ribs in batches for 3 to 4 minutes per side, until well browned. Transfer to a plate. Repeat with the remaining 2 tablespoons oil and the remaining ribs until they are all browned.

4 Pour off the excess fat from the pot. Add the reserved aromatics to the pot along with 1 teaspoon kosher salt and cook over medium heat for 5 minutes, or until the vegetables are soft. Add the tomato paste and stir for 2 minutes, or until the mixture is glossy. Add the reserved wine, bring to a boil, and reduce by half. This will take about 30 minutes.

5 Preheat the oven to 325°F.

6 Pour the chicken broth into the pot and add another teaspoon kosher salt. Taste the simmering braising liquid at this point for seasoning, adding more salt if needed. Return the short ribs to the pot, cover, and braise in the oven for 4 to 5 hours, basting regularly, until the meat is very tender. Remove from the oven and, if you have time, let the short ribs and braising liquid cool overnight in the refrigerator.

7 The next day, scrape off and remove any fat from the top. Remove the short ribs from the congealed liquid and put them in a shallow, medium pot.

Put the Dutch oven with the braising liquid over medium heat. When hot, strain the liquid over the short ribs. Gently heat the short ribs and liquid over medium heat until they are warmed through. If the bones have not already fallen from the meat on their own, give them a gentle pull and discard them now.

8 To serve, remove the braised meat to a serving platter and ladle the sauce over the top. Sprinkle with a little flaky sea salt and garnish with gremolata.

STEWED TRIPE WITH TOMATOES & OLIVES

Serves
6 *to* **8**

Tripe is the stomach lining of a cow, and when properly prepared, it can be really special. But for some reason, people tend to shy away from it. I don't remember eating tripe as a child, even though I was raised by a Greek-Sicilian mother. It wasn't until the early 1990s, when I was a chef at Giovanni's in Cleveland, that I was blown away by how delicious tripe could be. Tony Vella, a day chef there who made all the long-cook sauces and most braises, was killer at classic Italian food. Every once in a while, he would make a big pot of tripe. It wasn't our best seller, but it was with-out a doubt my favorite dish. Tony's secret was to boil the tripe twice in water with some vinegar, vanilla bean, and mirepoix, which made it milder. This is my version of Tony's amazing dish. It has nice heat from the pepper flakes, which goes great with the briny olives and fresh herbs.

TRIPE

2 pounds calf tripe

1 cup white wine vinegar

1 vanilla bean, split (optional)

2 bay leaves

1 red onion, quartered

6 garlic cloves, peeled

2 tablespoons red pepper flakes

2 large pinches of kosher salt

STEW

1 tablespoon olive oil

2 cups thinly sliced red onions

Kosher salt

2 garlic cloves, thinly sliced

½ cup dry white wine

1 (16-ounce) can San Marzano tomatoes, pureed with liquid

1 cup pitted green Sicilian olives, such as Castelvetrano

1 teaspoon red pepper flakes

½ cup fresh flat-leaf parsley leaves, sliced

½ cup fresh mint leaves, sliced

1 To prepare the tripe: Begin by rinsing the tripe thoroughly under cold water, and then put it in a large pot with enough water to cover. Add half of each of the remaining ingredients and bring to a boil. Remove the tripe from the pot and discard the liquid and aromatics. Return the blanched tripe to the pot, cover with fresh water, and add the remaining half of each of the ingredients. Bring to a boil and then reduce the heat so that the mixture simmers. Cook until the tripe is tender, about 4 hours.

2 Remove the tripe from the pot and let cool slightly. Discard the liquid and aromatics. Slice the tripe into 1-inch-wide strips.

3 To make the stew: In a 2-quart pot over medium-high heat, combine the olive oil, onions, and a pinch of salt and cook for 4 minutes. Add the garlic and cook for another minute. Add the tripe, white wine, and tomatoes and bring to simmer. Add the olives and red pepper flakes and simmer for 20 minutes. (The tripe can be cooled, covered, and refrigerated for up to 3 days. Reheat before serving.) Stir in the parsley and mint and serve.

DEREK'S SWEETBREADS

Derek Clayton has worked with me for years, first as chef at Lola and now as our group's corporate chef. He also is my right-hand man on *Iron Chef America.* I have never met a cook as thoughtful or as talented, and he's been making me look good for quite a while. This is one of my favorite dishes that he came up with. The combo may seem a little odd at first (and, yes, you do have to start this recipe two days ahead), but it is truly amazing and shows why I hold him in such high regard. Rich and savory, this dish is meant to be an occasional indulgence!

2 pounds veal sweetbreads

Kosher salt

1 large red onion, quartered

2 celery stalks, cut into large dice

1 cup large-diced leeks, white parts only

1 lemon, halved

1 teaspoon black peppercorns

1 bay leaf, fresh or dried

¼ cup canola oil

Soy-Dijon Glaze (recipe follows)

Rice flour, for dredging

Creamed Leeks (page 238), optional

Seared Wild Mushrooms (page 230)

Blue Cheese Sauce (recipe follows)

1 Two nights before you want to serve the sweetbreads, submerge them in salted ice water and refrigerate overnight. This begins the cleaning process, drawing out any impurities that may be left in the meat.

2 The following day, put a large pan over medium-high heat. Add the onion, celery, leeks, lemon, peppercorns, bay leaf, ¼ cup salt, and 4 quarts water and bring to a simmer. The poaching liquid should taste very salty at this point. Have ready an ice bath and set aside.

3 Meanwhile, drain the sweetbreads from their soaking liquid and put in a large bowl. Add 8 cups ice to the bowl. When the poaching liquid reaches a simmer, add the sweetbreads and ice and stir. The ice acts as a buffer that prevents the sweetbreads from cooking too quickly. The goal is to poach them slowly so they end up evenly cooked and creamy throughout. Lower the heat to medium-low and poach, stirring occasionally, for about 17 minutes. When done, the sweetbreads will turn pale white and feel somewhat firm. Remove from the poaching liquid and plunge into the prepared ice bath. Discard the poaching liquid.

4 When the sweetbreads are cool, drain them and remove the thin membrane that covers the whole organ. It should peel off easily using your fingers. When it is off, look for any pieces of solidified fat and remove them. You may have to break up the sweetbreads slightly to do so. When fully cleaned, arrange the sweetbreads in a single layer on a kitchen towel-lined rimmed baking sheet. Put another towel on top, followed by another baking sheet. Put a few heavy plates on top to evenly press the sweetbreads. Refrigerate overnight.

5 Have ready a rimmed baking sheet fitted with a rack. Heat a large sauté pan over medium-high heat. Add the oil. While the oil heats up, begin the breading process by first coating the sweetbreads in soy-Dijon glaze, then dredging them with rice flour. Shake off any excess flour and, working in

2 batches, put the pieces in the hot pan. Cook until very golden brown, about 2 minutes per side. Move them to the prepared baking sheet and lightly season with salt.

6 To serve, spoon the creamed leeks onto a large serving platter. Spoon the mushrooms over the top. Put the seared sweetbreads on top of that and then drizzle with some of the blue cheese sauce. All of the components to this dish can be made a day ahead and simply reheated over low heat while cooking the sweetbreads.

SOY-DIJON GLAZE *Makes about 1 cup*

½ cup soy sauce

½ cup Dijon or stadium-style mustard

3½ teaspoons hot mustard powder

Whisk together all the ingredients and set aside until ready to use.

BLUE CHEESE SAUCE *Makes 2 cups*

1 tablespoon olive oil

1 cup medium-diced red onion

½ cup medium-diced leek, white parts only

2 tablespoons sliced shallot

2 small garlic cloves, sliced

Kosher salt

1 cup dry white wine

1 quart chicken broth, preferably homemade (page 163), warmed

½ cup heavy cream

2 tablespoons cornstarch mixed with 2 tablespoons water

¼ cup crumbled buttermilk blue cheese

2 tablespoons finely chopped chives

1 Heat a large Dutch oven over medium heat. Add the olive oil. When the oil is hot, add the onion, leek, shallot, and garlic along with a pinch of salt. Cook for 4 minutes, or until softened, then add the white wine, and reduce until the pot is almost dry. Add the chicken broth and reduce by three-quarters. This stage may take up to 20 minutes. The sauce should thicken and brown slightly.

2 Pour in the cream and reduce by slightly more than half, about 10 minutes. Strain into a smaller saucepan, return to a light boil, and then whisk in the cornstarch and water mixture. Whisk in the blue cheese and then check and adjust for seasoning. Whisk in the chives.

SPARE RIBS

CENTER CUT
PORK LOIN CHOPS

PORK

BUTT

HOCKS

TROTTERS

PORK SHANKS

GROUND PORK

TENDERLOIN

BELLY (BACON)

As most of you know, I'm a huge fan of pork. It's not just because I find the meat absolutely delicious—which I do—but because the pig is the most versatile animal on the farm. There's good reason why chefs say that you can cook "everything but the squeal" on a pig. From nose to tail, the pig is nothing but good eats. Don't believe me? Well, consider the following: The belly gives us bacon, pancetta, and a million other tasty treats; the legs give rise to ham, prosciutto, and braised trotters; the ribs are amazing smoked and grilled, as is the shoulder; you can stuff and roast the hocks; you can cure the jowls into *guanciale*; fry the skin and you've got cracklings; fry the ears and you've got crispy goodness on a plate; render the lard and whatever you deep-fry in it will taste like heaven. And I haven't even gotten to chops, sausages, *salumis*, terrines, pâtés. . . .

HOW TO CHOOSE PORK

Pork is not "the other white meat," despite what people have been paid to try to convince us. That famous ad slogan had us believing that pork should be as lean as poultry. Thankfully, today's breeders are putting the fat—and thus the flavor—back into the pig. Wonderful heritage breeds like Berkshire, Tamworth, and Gloucestershire Old Spots are more consistently available than ever before, which is great news for us pork fans. The first time I cooked up some heritage hog for my grandfather, he looked at me and said, "That's how pork tasted when I was a kid."

If you can find heritage breed pork, start there. It may be more expensive than conventional meat, but, again, it's how pork should taste. If you can't find heritage pork, look for organic meat that has been raised without hormones or antibiotics. Pork should have a lovely pink or rosy color to it, not white, pale, and washed out. Make sure the fat is a rich, creamy white and not yellow or pink.

Some of the specific breeds that I enjoy include Duroc, Red Wattle, Tamworth, Gloucestershire Old Spots, Berkshire, and the more common Large Black. They are all fantastic and each has unique characteristics that I love for various reasons. The Duroc,

Berkshire, and Black are the most common of the bunch. They tend to be very consistent in their flavor, which I classify as mild. When I'm making bacon, I like the Tamworth because the bellies have even layers of fat. The Red Wattle tends to be the leanest of the breeds, but it makes up for it in deep pork flavor, perfect for grilled chops. I don't think you can go wrong with any well-raised heritage breed. Like most things, it comes down to use and personal preference. Buy, taste, and experiment your way through all of them.

When cooking pork, you don't have to cook it to death. We have been brainwashed to believe that we'll die if we eat a piece of pork that hasn't been burned past all recognition. In fact, the USDA just lowered the safe cooking temperatures for pork. For the leaner cuts of pork like chops and tenderloins, cook the meat to 140°F. By the time it has a chance to rest, it will get up to 145°F. Not only will the meat be safe to eat, it will actually be juicy and delicious, something we couldn't say about "the other white meat."

COOK IT RIGHT: PORK

Don't just stick with tried and true chops and ribs; give other cuts some love. Thanks to great natural marbling, most parts of the hog hold up well to braising, roasting, and smoking.

GRILL/PAN-ROAST/BROIL

» Tenderloin
» Rib chop
» Loin
» Loin chop

BRAISE

» Shank
» Butt (shoulder)
» Belly
» Tail

» Ears
» Cheeks
» Shoulder chops

OVEN-ROAST

» Belly
» Leg (ham)
» Rack

STEW

» Ears
» Shank

SMOKE

» Butt (shoulder)
» Leg (ham)
» Belly
» Shank
» Rack
» Cheeks
» Ribs

GRIND

» Belly
» Fatback
» Butt (shoulder)

Pork	Pork	Pork	Pork
Feet	Center Cut Chops	Grilling Chops	Butterfly Chops
$1.99/lb	$4.79/lb	$4.79/lb	$4.89/lb

| Pork Boneless Loin $4.89/lb | | Pork Tenderloin $5.99/lb | Pork/Veal City Chicken $5.99/lb | Pork Cutlet $4.39/lb |

PORK PIE

Pork pie is the perfect holiday dish. Not only is it delicious served hot out of the oven, but it is every bit as good warm or even at room temperature. That means you can bake it before the guests arrive, set it out when they do, and watch it vanish throughout the course of an evening. I would also like to add that pork pie makes great leftovers, but mine never seems to make it that long to know for certain.

8 ounces slab bacon, cut into medium dice

2 pounds ground pork

Kosher salt and freshly ground black pepper

1 cup chopped celery

2 cups chopped red onions

2 garlic cloves, chopped

1 pound russet potatoes, peeled and cut into large dice

½ cup chopped celery leaves

½ cup chopped fresh flat-leaf parsley

1 tablespoon chopped fresh savory

Pinch of ground cinnamon

Pinch of ground cloves

Pastry dough for 2 (8-inch) double-crust pies, homemade (page 68) or store-bought

1 large egg yolk beaten with 1 tablespoon milk

1 Put a large Dutch oven over medium heat. Add the bacon and cook until crisp, about 3 minutes. Remove the bacon from the pot and set aside on a plate. Add the ground pork to the pot drippings along with some salt and pepper, and brown for about 3 minutes. Remove the pork from the pot and set aside on the plate with the bacon.

2 Add the celery, onions, and garlic and cook for 5 minutes. Deglaze the pot with 1 cup water, scraping up the bits on the bottom with a wooden spoon. Return the pork and bacon to the pot along with the potatoes, celery leaves, parsley, savory, cinnamon, and cloves. Simmer for 20 minutes, or until all of the liquid has evaporated.

3 Preheat the oven to 400°F.

4 Meanwhile, roll out the chilled pie dough and prick all over with a fork. Line two 8-inch pie plates with half of the dough and refrigerate for 15 minutes.

5 Fill the pie plates with the meat mixture. Cover both pies with the top crusts, trimming and crimping the edges together to seal. Brush the tops with the egg yolk mixture and season with salt and pepper. Cut several steam vents in the center of each pie with a paring knife.

6 Bake the pies for 45 minutes to an hour, until the crusts are golden brown. Let cool for at least 30 minutes before serving.

PASTRY DOUGH *Makes enough for 2 (8-inch) double-crust pies*

6 cups all-purpose flour

2 teaspoons kosher salt

2 tablespoons sugar

1 pound unsalted butter, cold, diced

1½ to 2 cups ice water

Unless you are making the dough by hand, this recipe must be made in two batches. The bowl of a typical food processor is not large enough to accommodate a double batch.

1 Put half of the flour, salt, and sugar in the bowl of a food processor, pulsing a few times to mix. Add half of the butter. Pulse until the butter is about the size of small peas. With the machine running, begin adding the ice water a few tablespoons at a time (up to ¾ to 1 cup total) until the dough begins to form a ball. Stop adding water as soon as it does.

2 Dump the dough out onto a floured work surface and bring together into a ball. Divide the ball into 2 equal halves. Flatten each mound slightly, wrap in plastic wrap, and refrigerate for at least 30 minutes .

3 Repeat with the remaining ingredients. The dough will keep for up to 1 week in the fridge or up to 2 months in the freezer. Defrost overnight in the refrigerator before rolling.

PORCHETTA

Porchetta is a type of porky, herbed, garlicky, street-food goodness that you can find throughout Italy. It is fatty and loaded with flavor, making it perfect in a sandwich. It is just as good when served for dinner with some bitter greens like arugula or dandelion, dressed simply with fresh lemon juice and olive oil.

8 ounces pancetta, finely chopped

10 garlic cloves, minced

Grated zest of 3 lemons

Grated zest of 1 orange

½ cup chopped fresh flat-leaf parsley

Leaves from 4 sprigs fresh rosemary, chopped

2 tablespoons red pepper flakes

2 tablespoons rinsed capers, chopped

Kosher salt

1 (10- to 12-pound) skin-on boneless fresh ham, butterflied

1 Preheat the oven to 350°F.

2 Put the pancetta in the bowl of a food processor and pulse until it forms a paste. Transfer to a bowl and mix in by hand the garlic, citrus zests, parsley, rosemary, red pepper flakes, and capers and 2 tablespoons salt until thoroughly blended.

3 Put the ham flesh-side-up on a cutting board and score the meat with the tip of a sharp knife every inch or so in a cross-hatch pattern. Rub the pancetta paste into the meat, making sure to get it into the score marks. Flip the ham over and cross the skin with the knife as you did the flesh. Roll the ham up skin-side-out, and secure with kitchen twine. Season the skin lightly with salt.

4 Put the pork in a roasting pan and transfer to the oven to roast for 2 hours.

5 Increase the oven temperature to 400°F and roast until the pork reaches an internal temperature of 170°F and the skin is nice and crisp, about 1½ hours.

6 Remove from the oven and let rest for 30 minutes. Thinly slice the porchetta before serving. Don't worry if there are leftovers, as porchetta makes awesome sandwiches—hot or cold—and holds up well for days in the fridge.

SPICY PORK BURGER WITH MANCHEGO & POBLANOS

When it comes to burgers, beef is king. That said, there are times when even I like to mix things up a bit. This zesty recipe combines pork, one of my favorite meats, with moderately spicy ancho chile powder and roasted poblano peppers. These burgers are great in summer cooked over a hot charcoal grill. Pair them with a cold and hoppy IPA.

1 tablespoon ancho chile powder

1 garlic clove, chopped

1 shallot, chopped

2 jalapeños, with seeds and ribs, chopped

1 tablespoon kosher salt

½ teaspoon sugar

3 pounds pork butt, cubed

4 poblano peppers

8 slices Manchego cheese

8 brioche buns

Leaves from 1 bunch fresh cilantro

1 Mix together the chile powder, garlic, shallot, jalapeños, salt, and sugar in a gallon-sized zip-top bag. Add the pork, toss to coat with the seasonings, and refrigerate overnight.

2 Thoroughly chill all the sausage-grinding equipment and a medium mixing bowl. Grind the pork mixture through the small die into the chilled bowl. Mix the ground meat lightly with your hands and then bring it together to form a large ball. Divide the ball in half and then each half in quarters, to get 8 equal portions. Form each portion into a ½-inch-thick burger.

3 Heat a charcoal or gas grill to medium-high.

4 Grill the poblanos until blackened on all sides. Transfer to a bowl and cover with plastic wrap to steam for 5 to 10 minutes. Uncover the bowl, and then peel, halve, and seed the peppers.

5 Grill the burgers over medium-high heat for 3 minutes per side, or until they reach an internal temperature of 150°F. In order to develop a good crust, do not move the burgers until it's time to flip them. If the grill begins to flare up, put the lid on for the remaining time.

6 When the burgers are almost done, top each one with a piece of cheese and put the lid on for about 1 minute to melt the cheese. Remove the burgers to a plate to rest for a couple of minutes.

7 Meanwhile, split and toast the buns, being careful not to burn them.

8 To assemble the burgers, put a piece of roasted poblano on the bottom of each bun half. Put the burger with cheese on top, followed by some cilantro. Top with the other half of the bun and enjoy!

SMOKED PORK CHOPS

We have been serving smoked pork chops at Lola since day one; they are one of our signature dishes. We pair them with Soft Polenta with Aged Cheddar (page 248) and a pickled chile salad. This recipe employs the same technique as the one we use at the restaurant, but at home, I like to top this version with Pickled Shallots (page 222). If you don't have the time or gear to smoke the chops, they're still quite tasty simply grilled.

1 dried ancho chile, torn and ground

2 tablespoons sugar

1½ teaspoons coriander seeds, toasted and ground

1½ teaspoons cumin seeds, toasted and ground

⅛ teaspoon red pepper flakes

Kosher salt and freshly ground black pepper

1 (8-bone) rack of pork

2 tablespoons olive oil

1 Combine the ancho powder, sugar, coriander, cumin, red pepper flakes, 2 tablespoons salt, and ¼ teaspoon black pepper and rub into all sides of the rack. Put the pork on a plate, cover, and refrigerate to cure overnight.

2 Prepare and set a smoker to 150°F, using apple-wood chips.

3 Rinse the pork under cold water. Pat it dry and put it on a roasting-rack-lined sheet tray. Put it in the smoker and smoke for about 1 hour. Remove the pork from the smoker and put it in the refrigerator to cool.

4 Heat a charcoal or gas grill to medium-high. Remove the pork from the fridge 10 minutes prior to grilling and cut into 8 chops.

5 Brush the chops with olive oil and lightly season with salt and freshly ground black pepper. You do not need a lot of seasoning because of the cure. Grill the chops for about 5 minutes per side, or until they reach an internal temperature of 140°F. Remove the chops from the grill and let rest for 5 minutes before serving.

HOUSE BACON

Yes, it's true: Everything is better with bacon! Anthony Bourdain recently wrote that he wished the bacon fad would come to an end. Uh, Tony! Bacon is like a good pair of Levi's—it never goes out of style. Not even Denny's doing their best to screw it up could end my love affair with bacon. While there are some great artisanal bacons on the market, bacon is so easy to make at home, you should give it a try. And by mixing and matching your favorite herbs and spices, you can customize this recipe to suit your own taste. Custom bacon—how cool is that?

3 tablespoons kosher salt

1 teaspoon pink curing salt

1½ tablespoons packed dark brown sugar

6 pounds fresh pork belly

1 Mix the kosher salt, pink curing salt, and brown sugar. Thoroughly coat the pork belly with this mixture, making sure to use it all. Put the belly on a rimmed baking sheet and cover it with a piece of parchment paper. Put another baking sheet on top of the belly and weight it down with a few heavy cans or plates. Put it in the refrigerator to cure for 7 days.

2 Rinse the pork belly in cold water and put it on a baking sheet lined with a rack. Refrigerate the belly, uncovered, overnight to dry it out a bit.

3 Prepare and set a smoker to 200°F. Using apple-wood chips, smoke the pork belly for 1 hour. Continue cooking the belly in the smoker, without smoke, until it reaches an internal temperature of 160°F, about 3 hours.

4 When the bacon is done, remove it from the smoker and refrigerate for several hours. It will keep for 1 week in the refrigerator or up to 2 months in the freezer.

GRILLED PORK TENDERLOIN

While I generally find tenderloin to be the least flavorful cut of an animal, I do give pork tenderloin a free pass thanks to its more naturally fatty composition. But even in the case of pork tenderloin, which is on the low end of the flavor spectrum, the cut needs to be woken up a bit. I season these tenderloins pretty liberally before grilling and then serve topped with Mustard Fruit (page 226), which I always have stashed in the fridge.

1 tablespoon Dijon mustard

2 teaspoons kosher salt

2 teaspoons coriander seeds, toasted and ground

2 teaspoons cumin seeds, toasted and ground

1 teaspoon smoked paprika

Grated zest of 1 lime

½ cup chopped fresh cilantro

2 pork tenderloins (about 4 pounds total), trimmed of silver skin

1 cup arugula

1 tablespoon extra-virgin olive oil

1 Combine the mustard, salt, coriander, cumin, paprika, lime zest, and cilantro in a large zip-top bag and add the tenderloins. Shake the bag to coat the pork, and refrigerate overnight or for up to 2 days.

2 Heat a charcoal or gas grill to medium-high. Remove the pork from the fridge 10 minutes prior to grilling.

3 Grill the tenderloins until medium, about 4 minutes per side. Remove from the grill to a cutting board and let rest for 5 minutes. Slice the tenderloins and arrange on a platter. Top with the arugula and drizzle the arugula with the olive oil.

GRILLING

What is it about grilling that turns men—who are perfectly happy staying out of the kitchen—into crazy-eyed cooks? Sadly, many men (and women) get it wrong. Like a lot of cooking techniques, simply following a few basic tips can turn you into a grillmaster.

For starters, take the meat out of the fridge with enough time to come to room temperature. This will help the meat to cook more evenly. Make sure the grill grates are clean and oiled or else the meat will stick. Have everything you need ready before getting started. That includes a good pair of restaurant-style tongs (not those long goofy ones that come in fancy grill sets), a spray bottle of water to snuff out flash fires, a pastry brush if basting meat with glazes or sauces, and a clean platter and piece of foil for when the food is done.

When it comes to fuel, I go for the smoky goodness of a real live fire. My first choice is real lump charcoal, which burns hotter than gas. I also grill over hardwood, or, failing all of the above, good-quality briquettes. Gas, or what I like to call the lazy man's grill, is my last choice. When arranging the hot coals or wood embers, it's key to create a hot zone and a cool zone. Meat is seared in the hot zone in the beginning of the cooking process and moved to the cool side to finish. The grill stays open for the searing portion and then is closed while the meat finishes.

Now, put the meat on the hot side of the grill—*and leave it alone!* Just because you're bored doesn't mean you need to poke, flip, press, or otherwise pester the meat. Instead of a timer, I use a beer to judge how long to leave it. Usually, when I've polished off half the bottle, it's time to flip. When I've killed the whole bottle, it's time to move the meat to the cool side, baste it, and cover the grill. What we're looking for is a good char—not burn—on both sides. When the meat reaches your desired doneness, remove it from the grill, put it on the platter, cover it with the foil, *and leave it alone!* Allowing the meat to rest for at least 10 minutes after cooking is one of the easiest and most important steps of all. Bored? Have another beer.

SMOKED HAM

While glazed hams may be time-honored centerpieces at American holiday celebrations, I can't help myself from cooking them year-round. The beauty of doing it yourself—in addition to the leftovers—is knowing that your ham will be free of nitrates and other junk that ends up in some brands. Although this ham will not sport the unnatural pink hue we have come to expect, it *will* pack twice the flavor of the store-bought stuff—and you won't have to wait in line!

2 cups kosher salt

1 cup packed light brown sugar

1 head garlic, halved crosswise

2 tablespoons mustard seeds

2 tablespoons coriander seeds

3 bay leaves, fresh or dried

1 bone-in, skin on fresh ham (about 20 pounds)

1 cup honey

1 cup Dijon mustard

2 tablespoons chopped fresh rosemary

1 In a large pot, combine 2 gallons water, the salt, brown sugar, garlic, mustard seeds, coriander seeds, and bay leaves and bring to a simmer over high heat. Whisk until the salt and sugar are completely dissolved. Remove from the heat and let cool.

2 In a container large enough to hold the ham, completely submerge the ham in the cooled brine. Weight down the ham with a heavy plate if necessary to keep it fully submerged. Brine in the refrigerator for 7 days.

3 Remove the ham from the brine and discard the brine. Put the ham on a rimmed baking sheet lined with a roasting rack, and let the ham air-dry overnight, uncovered, in the fridge.

4 Prepare and set a smoker to 200°F, using apple-wood chips.

5 Put the ham in the smoker and let it go for 4 hours, replenishing the chips halfway through cooking.

6 Whisk together the honey, mustard, and rosemary. Brush the ham with half of the glaze and return it to the smoker for another 3 to 4 hours, until it reaches an internal temperature of 165°F.

7 Remove the ham from the smoker and brush with the remaining glaze. Let cool. You can serve this ham sliced cold or reheat it in a 250°F oven until warm in the center before slicing.

SMOKED PORK BUTT WITH HABANERO GLAZE

There are few joys in life greater than pulled pork. As soon as summer hits, the first thing I do is grab my smoker and get a big, old pork butt going. While Midwesterners tend to favor thick and sweet barbecue sauces, I much prefer the thinner vinegar-style sauces of the South. The acid really wakes up the pork and cuts through—and complements—all the fatty, smoky heavenliness. Almost nothing makes me smile like pulled pork on a soft bun topped with slaw and pickles!

PORK BUTT

2 tablespoons kosher salt

2 teaspoons cracked black peppercorns

2 teaspoons coriander seeds, toasted and ground

1 teaspoon cumin seeds, toasted and ground

½ teaspoon garlic powder

1 bone-in pork butt (about 5 pounds)

HABANERO GLAZE

1 gallon orange juice, not from concentrate

½ cup fresh lime juice

1 habanero chile, with a slit cut in 1 side

1 cup packed light brown sugar

Cleveland BBQ Sauce (page 100) or other barbecue sauce

1 To prepare the pork butt: Combine the salt, pepper, coriander, cumin, and garlic powder and rub all over the pork. Cover and refrigerate overnight.

2 To make the glaze: Put all of the glaze ingredients in a large nonreactive saucepan over medium-high heat and boil until reduced by half. This will take about an hour.

3 Meanwhile, prepare and set a smoker to 225°F, using apple-wood chips.

4 Put the pork butt in the smoker and let it go for 2 hours.

5 Brush the pork with some of the glaze. Continue to smoke the pork, brushing it with the glaze every 45 minutes, until it reaches an internal temperature of 170°F. While it usually takes me about 6 hours total to smoke a pork butt perfectly, occasionally a cold beer or two gets in the way of my temperature-monitoring duties. This could extend or reduce the time it takes to smoke the pork. Either way, remember to relax and be patient.

6 Remove the pork from the smoker and let rest for about 30 minutes. Using two forks, shred the meat into long, thin strands and toss with the barbecue sauce.

PK'S PORK CRACKLINGS

Serves
6

Paul Kahan—aka PK—is one of my favorite American chefs. His passion, attention to detail, and dedication in the kitchen are unmatched. The first time I ate at Publican, one of his restaurants in Chicago, he dropped off a bag of house-made pork rinds. It was pork ecstasy! They were like crispy pillows of puffy pork goodness. I immediately dragged PK back to the kitchen to show me how he made them. This is my version of his incredible cracklings.

1 pound pork skin

Peanut oil, for deep-frying

Kosher salt

1 Cut the pork skin into 4 pieces. It will cook more evenly and be easier to clean later on.

2 In a large saucepan over medium heat, bring 4 quarts water to a simmer. Add the skins and cook for 1 hour, or until they are soft and somewhat gelatinous.

3 Preheat the oven to 300°F.

4 Remove the skins from the water with a slotted spoon and put onto a large plate. Discard the liquid. Let the skins cool in the refrigerator for at least 15 minutes so they will be easier to handle.

5 Put one of the pieces on a cutting board skin-side-down. The other side will have bits of meat and fat on it that will have turned white during cooking. With a very sharp chef's knife, slice as much of the meat and fat off as possible, leaving only a thin piece of skin. Be careful not to slice into the skin underneath. The cleaner you get the skin, the crispier the crackling will be when fried. Repeat with the remaining pieces.

6 Arrange the skins on a parchment-paper- or Silpat-lined sheet tray and put in the oven for 1½ hours. Flip the skins and continue cooking for 1½ hours, or until the skins are completely dry. Remove from the oven and let cool.

7 When cool enough to handle, scrape off any remaining bits of fat and meat. The back of a knife works well for this. At this point, the cracklings can be stored in an airtight container for up to 1 week.

8 Heat about 4 inches of oil in a deep-fryer or pot to 350°F. Break the cracklings into small, inch-sized pieces. Fry in batches for 30 to 45 seconds, until crisp and puffy. Remove from the oil and season with salt. Serve immediately.

PORK & BEANS

Just because this is an incredibly humble dish doesn't mean that it won't bring huge smiles to the faces of your guests. Unlike many of the pork and beans recipes out there that tend to be too sweet and primarily served as a side dish, this one is a savory version. That makes it perfect as a wintertime main course. It also reheats well.

1 pound dried navy beans

1 pound bacon, homemade (page 75) or store-bought slab, cut into large dice

2 cups small-diced peeled carrots

1 cup small-diced red onion

6 garlic cloves, sliced

4 links of sweet Italian sausage, homemade (page 87) or store-bought, cut in half

1 (28-ounce) can San Marzano chopped tomatoes

1 smoked ham hock, homemade (page 86) or store-bought

3 sprigs fresh rosemary

2 bay leaves, preferably fresh

1 quart chicken or pork broth, preferably homemade (page 163 or page 96)

Kosher salt and freshly ground black pepper

1 cup plain dried bread crumbs

½ cup chopped fresh flat-leaf parsley

¼ cup chopped fresh chives

1 Soak the beans overnight in enough water to cover them by at least 2 inches.

2 Drain the beans and transfer to a large saucepan. Add enough water to cover by 2 inches and bring to a simmer. Cook for about 1 hour, or until slightly tender. Remove from the heat and set aside for the beans to cool in their cooking liquid.

3 Preheat the oven to 375°F.

4 In a large Dutch oven set over medium heat, slowly cook the bacon until just crisp, about 5 minutes. Remove the bacon from the pot and set aside on a plate. Add the carrots, onion, and garlic to the drippings in the pot and cook for 3 to 4 minutes. Remove from the pot and set aside on the plate with the bacon. Turn the heat up to medium-high and add the sausage. When the sausage is browned on all sides, about 8 to 10 minutes, return the bacon and vegetables to the pot, along with the tomatoes, ham hock, rosemary, bay leaves, and chicken broth. Simmer for 5 minutes.

5 Drain the beans and add them to the pot. Discard the bean cooking liquid. Taste the sausage mixture and adjust for seasoning, adding salt and pepper as needed. Bring the mixture back up to a simmer, stirring to incorporate the beans. Transfer to the oven and cook, uncovered, for 1 hour.

6 Pick out and discard the bay leaves. Combine the bread crumbs, parsley, and chives. Sprinkle the mixture on top of the beans. The beans should be slightly thickened by now. Bake for 20 minutes, or until the bread crumbs are golden brown. Serve hot.

PIG TROTTERS WITH APPLE & CELERY ROOT SALAD

Serves
6

The poor pig trotter gets no respect—this despite the fact that it's incredibly affordable, it's rich in flavor, and it has a gelatinous quality that makes it great in soups and stews. Sure, it takes a little work to pull the meat off the bones, but, man, is it worth the effort. In this recipe, I pair the humble trotter with an equally humble crunchy apple and celery root salad. One bite of this and you may never go back to those boring chicken Caesars again!

3 pig trotters

Kosher salt

1 cup dry white wine

¼ cup white wine vinegar

1 medium red onion, quartered

1 cup roughly chopped peeled carrots

1 bunch celery, roughly chopped

2 bay leaves, preferably fresh

4 garlic cloves, unpeeled, smashed

6 sprigs fresh thyme

1 tablespoon black peppercorns

1 tablespoon mustard seeds

Apple & Celery Root Salad (page 209)

1 Soak the trotters in salted ice water for a couple of hours. This will remove any impurities that may be lingering. Remove the trotters from the salt water and rinse well.

2 Put the trotters, wine, vinegar, onion, carrots, celery, bay leaves, garlic, thyme, 2 tablespoons salt, the peppercorns, and mustard seeds in a large pot and cover with water. Weight down the contents with a heavy plate to keep everything submerged. Bring to a simmer and cook until the trotters are tender, about 3 hours. Carefully remove the trotters from the pot with a slotted spoon and set aside to cool. Strain the cooking liquid and reserve it for use in another recipe (such as Pork & Beans, opposite).

3 When the trotters are cool enough to handle, remove as much meat as possible from the bones with your hands or using two forks. This may take a while because you'll probably have to rinse the sticky gelatin off your hands frequently. You should end up with about 2 cups meat. (You can reserve the skin to fry up as cracklings—see page 82—to add to salads or eat as a late-night snack.)

4 Divide the salad among 6 plates and top with the trotter meat.

SMOKED HAM HOCKS

Ham hocks are a great way to give a flavor boost to soups, greens, or Pork & Beans (page 84), so I always try to keep some on hand; they keep for months in the freezer. I don't usually brine meats, but the technique works very well when smoking tough cuts like ham hocks.

2 cups kosher salt

5 teaspoons pink curing salt

2 cups sugar

2 bay leaves, fresh or dried

2 tablespoons coriander seeds, toasted

2 tablespoons black peppercorns

1 jalapeño, split lengthwise

1 head garlic, split crosswise

12 fresh ham hocks

1 In a large nonreactive pot, combine the kosher salt, pink curing salt, sugar, bay leaves, coriander, peppercorns, jalapeño, and garlic with 2 gallons water and bring to a simmer over high heat. Whisk to dissolve the salt and sugar. Remove from the heat and let cool. Pour the cooled brine into a 12-quart container and add the ham hocks, weighting them down with a heavy plate to keep them fully submerged. Refrigerate for 3 days.

2 Prepare and set a smoker to 200°F, using apple-wood chips.

3 Remove the hocks from the brine, pat them dry, and arrange on a baking sheet lined with a rack. Discard the brine. Smoke the hocks until they reach an internal temperature of 160°F. This will take 3½ to 4 hours.

4 Remove the hocks from the smoker and let cool in the refrigerator. Smoked hocks will keep for up to 2 weeks in the refrigerator and for several months in the freezer.

BRINING

To brine or not to brine, that is the question. The good news is that there's no wrong answer—it's just a matter of preference. Personally, I'm not a fan of brining because of what it does to the texture of the meat. As the liquid enters the cells, it kind of puffs up, or expands, the meat. When it is cooked, all that moisture is released, resulting in a texture that's too flabby for my liking. Brining became popular a few decades ago, when it was a lot harder to find quality meats with good marbling. Today, it's so much easier to find great meat, like well-raised heritage breeds that possess the proper amount of fat. I'd much rather slap on a quick cure (see page 40) the day before cooking, which enhances the flavor without sacrificing the texture. My one big exception to the no-brining rule is when I'm smoking meat for a long time, as in the case of Smoked Ham (page 78).

SWEET ITALIAN SAUSAGE

Makes
4
pounds

Of all the sausages out there, this is the one that most reminds me of my childhood. My mom would often add it to her sauces, both for spaghetti and lasagna, which gave them such wonderful richness and a slight kiss of fennel. And every summer when we went to the Feast of the Assumption celebration in Cleveland's Little Italy neighborhood, the very first thing I'd eat was a sweet Italian sausage–and–pepper sandwich. So good!

3 pounds boneless pork shoulder, cut into 1-inch cubes

1 pound fatback, cut into 1-inch cubes

3 tablespoons kosher salt

1 tablespoon sugar

3 garlic cloves, minced

1 large shallot, minced

½ cup chopped fresh flat-leaf parsley

2 tablespoons chopped fresh oregano

2 tablespoons fennel seeds, toasted

1 teaspoon freshly ground black pepper

½ cup ice water

Grated zest of 2 lemons

Juice of 1 lemon

6 feet of hog casing, soaked overnight and rinsed (see page 35), optional

1 Combine the pork shoulder, fatback, salt, sugar, garlic, shallot, parsley, oregano, fennel, and pepper in a gallon-sized zip-top bag and refrigerate overnight or for up to 2 days.

2 Thoroughly chill all the sausage-grinding equipment, the mixing bowl, and the paddle attachment. Grind the pork mixture through the medium-sized die onto a baking sheet. Refrigerate for 30 minutes to chill. When thoroughly chilled, put the ground pork in the mixing bowl and fit the mixer with the paddle attachment. Add the ice water, lemon zest, and lemon juice and blend on medium for about 1 minute. Return to the refrigerator until ready to use or for up to 3 days (or freeze for up to 1 month; defrost before proceeding).

3 Stuff this sausage filling into a hog casing (see page 36) and poach in simmering water or grill until the sausages reach an internal temperature of 155°F; form it into patties and pan-roast until browned and cooked through; or leave it loose to crumble into your favorite long-simmered pasta sauces.

LIVERWURST

Liverwurst is great to serve at a party slathered onto grilled bread and topped with shaved onions, celery leaves, and mustard. This sausage recipe is pretty easy to make. The hardest part will likely be sourcing the pork livers, but with a little advance notice your butcher or grocery store should be able to supply it. Casings are available online and at some sausage supply stores.

3 tablespoons dry milk powder

1 teaspoon sugar

2 teaspoons paprika

½ teaspoon fresh marjoram

1 teaspoon coriander seeds, toasted and ground

¼ teaspoon ground nutmeg

¼ teaspoon ground allspice

¼ teaspoon ground cinnamon

1½ teaspoons kosher salt, plus more for cooking

1 teaspoon ground white pepper

1 pound fresh pork liver, cubed

12 ounces lean pork butt, cubed

4 ounces fatback, cubed

1 large sweet white onion, finely diced

3 feet of hog-bung-style casing, soaked overnight and rinsed (see page 35)

Grilled bread, thinly sliced onion, celery leaves, and mustard, for serving

1 Combine the dry milk powder, sugar, paprika, marjoram, coriander, nutmeg, allspice, cinnamon, the 1½ teaspoons salt, and the pepper in a gallon-sized zip-top bag. Add the pork liver, pork butt, fatback, and diced sweet onion, mix to distribute the seasonings, and refrigerate overnight.

2 Thoroughly chill all the sausage-grinding equipment and the mixing bowl. Grind the chilled meat mixture through the small-sized die into the chilled mixing bowl. Mix thoroughly with your hands and then refrigerate for 30 minutes. Grind through the small die again, followed by another 30-minute chill. Repeat this process one more time for a total of 3 grindings and chill periods.

3 Stuff the ground meat into the casing (see page 36). Refrigerate for up to 5 days or freeze for up to 1 month. Defrost overnight before cooking.

4 To cook, fill a large pot with enough water to cover the liverwurst by at least 3 inches; bring to a boil and add salt. Add the sausage, weighting it down with a small plate so it stays submerged. When the water returns to a boil, reduce the heat so that the water barely simmers. Cook for 3 hours. Remove the liverwurst from the water and let cool. Refrigerate until ready to eat or for up to 2 days.

5 To serve, remove the casing and spread the liverwurst onto grilled bread. Garnish with sliced onion, celery leaves, and mustard.

CHORIZO

When I was chef at Cleveland's Piccolo Mondo in the early 1990s, we made all of our sausages in-house from scratch. While I was very familiar with most of the Italian sausages, I had never attempted chorizo. This recipe for fresh chorizo is the one we developed at that restaurant, and the one we still make and use at my restaurant Lolita. This zesty sausage is as much a crowd-pleaser today as it was back in the nineties. We use it loose in our spicy Mussels with Chorizo (page 107). Try it with eggs for breakfast!

3 pounds boneless pork shoulder, cut into 1-inch cubes

1 pound fatback, cut into 1-inch cubes

1 (3-ounce) can chipotles in adobo sauce, pureed with sauce

¼ cup cider vinegar

8 scallions, white parts only, thinly sliced

6 garlic cloves, minced

½ cup chopped fresh cilantro

2 tablespoons coriander seeds, toasted and ground

2 tablespoons cumin seeds, toasted and ground

1 tablespoon dried Mexican oregano

1 teaspoon smoked paprika

½ teaspoon ground cinnamon

¼ teaspoon ground allspice

2 tablespoons kosher salt

1 teaspoon freshly ground black pepper

1 tablespoon sugar

6 feet of hog casing, soaked overnight and rinsed (see page 35), optional

1 Combine all of the ingredients (except the hog casing) in a zip-top bag and refrigerate overnight or for up to 2 days.

2 Thoroughly chill all the sausage-grinding equipment, the mixing bowl, and the paddle attachment.

3 Grind the pork mixture through the medium-sized die into the mixing bowl. Refrigerate for 30 minutes to chill.

4 Blend on medium-high with the paddle attachment for 1 minute. Return to the refrigerator to chill for at least 30 minutes or up to 2 days (or freeze for up to 2 months; defrost before proceeding). Stuff the chorizo filling into a hog casing (see page 36) and poach in simmering water or grill until the sausage reaches an internal temperature of 155°F; form into patties and pan-roast until browned and cooked through; or leave it loose to crumble and cook in other recipes.

ELVIS BISCUITS WITH PEPPER GRAVY

Back in my youth, when I used to do a little more late-night partying, I'd occasionally wake up with an annoying morning hangover. Go figure, right? The one thing that eased the pain faster than anything else was a substantial breakfast that combined my sister-in-law Marilyn's "Elvis" biscuits and my wife Lizzie's pepper gravy. Turns out, the biscuits are super easy to assemble and the gravy is a breeze, and, hangover or not, this will always be a go-to breakfast at the Symon house.

GRAVY

¼ cup rendered bacon fat

1 cup minced red onion

Kosher salt

1 pound ground pork

2 tablespoons chopped fresh sage

1 teaspoon red pepper flakes

Freshly ground black pepper

¼ cup all-purpose flour

3 cups whole milk

BISCUITS

4 ounces lard, cubed, plus 2 tablespoons melted

2 cups cake flour

2 teaspoons baking powder

½ teaspoon baking soda

½ teaspoon kosher salt

¾ cup buttermilk

1 To make the gravy: Heat the bacon fat in a 4-quart saucepan over medium-high heat. Add the onion and a pinch of salt and cook, without coloring, for 3 minutes. Turn the heat up to high and add the pork, breaking it up into small pieces. Add 1 tablespoon of the sage, the red pepper flakes, 1 teaspoon salt, and 1 teaspoon black pepper. Brown the pork, turning occasionally, for about 5 minutes.

2 Add the flour, which will help thicken the sauce. Cook, stirring, for 1 minute and then add the milk, whisking to incorporate it. Bring the mixture to a boil, reduce the heat so that it simmers, and cook for 30 minutes, stirring occasionally.

3 Meanwhile, make the biscuits: Preheat the oven to 400°F. Brush a baking sheet with the 2 tablespoons melted lard.

4 In a large bowl, combine the cake flour, baking powder, baking soda, and salt. Add the cubed lard and blend the mixture by hand, crushing it between your fingertips, as if you were making pie dough. Continue mixing while adding the buttermilk. Make sure not to overwork the dough.

5 Drop the biscuits with a spoon onto the prepared baking sheet, leaving space between each one. You should have 12 biscuits, each about the size of a peach. Bake until lightly browned, about 15 minutes.

6 To finish the gravy and serve: Stir in the remaining 1 tablespoon sage, 1 teaspoon salt, and ½ teaspoon black pepper. Put 2 biscuits on each of 6 plates and ladle the gravy over the top of the hot biscuits.

BRAISED PORK SHANKS

When autumn turns to winter, you can bet that this dish will be showing up on Lola's menu. Like most braises, it's relatively easy to make, but it takes its time in the oven—perfect for a lazy Sunday supper with friends. Because the shanks come out so rich and tender, this dish really benefits from a bright and crunchy topper like Shaved Brussels Sprouts (page 216).

BRINE

1 cup kosher salt

½ cup sugar

1 head garlic, halved crosswise

2 sprigs fresh rosemary

1 tablespoon black peppercorns

1 tablespoon coriander seeds

1 bay leaf, fresh or dried

6 pork shanks

BRAISE

Canola oil

All-purpose flour, for dredging

3 cups roughly chopped red onions

3 cups roughly chopped celery

2 cups roughly chopped carrots

3 garlic cloves, unpeeled, smashed

Kosher salt

1 sprig fresh rosemary

Small bundle of fresh thyme

2 cups dry white wine

2 cups apple cider

4 quarts chicken broth, preferably homemade (page 163)

1 To brine the shanks: In a large nonreactive pot over high heat, combine the salt, sugar, garlic, rosemary, peppercorns, coriander seeds, and bay leaf with 4 quarts water and bring to a simmer. Whisk until the salt and sugar are completely dissolved. Remove from the heat and let cool.

2 In a container large enough to hold the shanks, completely submerge the pork in the cooled brine. Weight down the shanks with a heavy plate if necessary to keep them fully submerged. Refrigerate overnight.

3 To braise the shanks: Preheat the oven to 300°F.

4 Remove the shanks from the brine, discarding the liquid, and pat them dry. Heat a large Dutch oven over medium-high heat. Pour in enough canola oil to completely coat the bottom of the pot. Dredge the shanks with flour, shaking off any excess. In batches, brown the shanks, cooking for a few minutes on each side. As the shanks are browned, transfer to a plate.

5 Pour off all but 2 or 3 tablespoons of fat from the pot. Add the onions, celery, carrots, and garlic cloves along with a large pinch of salt. Cook the vegetables over medium heat, stirring from time to time, until tender, about 7 minutes. Add the rosemary and thyme and cook for another minute. Deglaze the pot with the white wine and simmer to reduce by three-quarters. Add the apple cider and let it reduce by half. Add the chicken broth and bring the braising liquid up to a simmer. Taste and adjust for seasoning.

6 Return the shanks to the pot, cover, and put in the oven until the meat is tender, 4 to 5 hours. Transfer the shanks from the braising pot to a clean pot. Strain the braising liquid over the shanks, discarding the solids. (If you have time, let the shanks cool in their liquid and then cover and refrigerate overnight. Discard any fat from the top before reheating.)

7 To serve, reheat the shanks in their braising liquid. Put the shanks on a platter and spoon some sauce on top.

HEAD CHEESE

Head cheese is definitely one delicacy that would benefit greatly from a more appetizing name. When we put it on the charcuterie boards at Lola, people devour it. But when we try and sell it on its own, most people wouldn't touch it with a ten-foot pole. Maybe we should call it pork loaf! Regardless of what it's called, I highly recommend giving it a try. It's inexpensive to make, it uses overlooked parts of the pig, and it's freaking delicious! While pig heads and tongues are not readily available at all grocery stores, they can be picked up or specially ordered from fine butcher shops.

1 pig head (about 7 pounds)

3 pig trotters

1 smoked ham hock, homemade (page 86) or store-bought

1 pork tongue

2 cups dry white wine

2 tablespoons red wine vinegar

2 teaspoons red pepper flakes

2 teaspoons coriander seeds, toasted

1 teaspoon mustard seeds

1 medium onion, quartered

8 garlic cloves, unpeeled, smashed

8 bay leaves, preferably fresh

1 small bunch fresh thyme (tied with kitchen twine)

2 tablespoons kosher salt

Crusty bread, sliced radishes, and grainy mustard, for serving

1 Get out your largest nonreactive pot. Put all of the head cheese ingredients in the pot and add enough water to cover by 2 or 3 inches. Weight down the contents with a small, heavy plate to keep everything submerged. Bring to a very low simmer on the stovetop. Cook for 3 hours.

2 Pull out the trotters, hock, and tongue. They should be very tender and almost falling apart. Put them on a plate to cool while the head continues to cook for another 2 hours. The head is ready when the jaw moves easily and the meat is tender to the touch. Remove the head to a baking sheet to cool slightly.

3 Meanwhile, strain the cooking liquid (discarding the solids), return it to the pot over high heat, and reduce the liquid by about half. This should yield about 5 quarts. Set aside 2½ cups for this recipe and let cool. Reserve the rest to use as stock. (It will keep for up to 1 week in the fridge and 2 months in the freezer.)

4 Remove all of the meat that you can from the head, hock, and trotters. Discard all of the skin, fat, and bones. Peel the membranes off the tongue. Do your best not to eat all the good parts now. Be patient; you'll be rewarded soon enough!

5 Cut all the meat into ¼-inch dice and mix to combine. You should end up with about 8 cups diced meat. Line an 11 by 3-inch ceramic terrine mold with plastic wrap, using enough to drape over the sides. Put the meat in a large bowl and mix in 1 cup of the cooled cooking liquid. Begin packing this mixture into the terrine until the halfway point. Firmly press the meat into the mold—you want it to be nice and snug. Slowly pour another cup of the cooking liquid on top, letting it seep in. Pack the rest of the meat into the mold, filling it all the way to the top and pressing it down firmly. Slowly pour in the remaining ½ cup cooking liquid.

6 Bring the plastic wrap that is hanging over the sides up and over the top to cover the meat. Put the terrine on a rimmed baking sheet, weighting down the top of the mold with cans or a heavy plate. Refrigerate overnight to set.

7 Peel back the plastic wrap from the top, flip the terrine over onto a cutting board, and unmold. Slice and serve with some good crusty bread, radishes, and grainy mustard. Just don't tell your friends it's called head cheese!

RIBS WITH CLEVELAND BBQ SAUCE

Here are my thoughts on ribs and what I believe makes them come out great. Most important, they must be smoked—not boiled, not baked, not braised—end of discussion. Second, I prefer St. Louis–style ribs over spare and even much-loved baby backs; to me, they just taste so much better. And finally, a properly cooked rib is not *fall-off-the-bone tender* as we have been led to believe. Ribs should have some fight left in them, firm enough to require a gentle tug to get the meat off the bone. To tell if a rib has been properly smoked, take a bite and look for the tell-tale pink smoke ring. Got it? Good! Now, let's get smokin'!

4 slabs St. Louis–style ribs

¼ cup cider vinegar

4 teaspoons kosher salt

1 teaspoon sugar

1 teaspoon sweet paprika

1 teaspoon garlic powder

1 teaspoon onion powder

1 teaspoon dried oregano

1 teaspoon coriander seeds, toasted and ground

1 teaspoon cumin seeds, toasted and ground

1 teaspoon chipotle powder

1 cup Cleveland BBQ Sauce (page 100) or your favorite barbecue sauce, plus more if needed

1 Brush both sides of the ribs with the vinegar. Thoroughly combine the salt, sugar, paprika, garlic powder, onion powder, oregano, coriander, cumin, and chipotle powder and liberally rub this mixture onto all sides of the ribs. I actually find this meat massage pretty relaxing. Cover the ribs and put in the fridge overnight to marinate.

2 Prepare and set a smoker to 225°F, using apple-wood chips.

3 Put the ribs in the smoker and cook for about 4 hours, or until tender.

4 Baste the ribs with the barbecue sauce and continue cooking for 30 minutes, or until the ribs get good and glazed.

5 To serve, cut the slabs into double or triple ribs. If you are not going to eat the ribs immediately, let them cool before wrapping them up and storing them in the fridge. When ready to enjoy, reheat the ribs on a hot grill, basting them near the end with more barbecue sauce.

CLEVELAND BBQ SAUCE *Makes about 2 cups*

1½ teaspoons olive oil

½ cup minced red onion

1 garlic clove, minced

Kosher salt

1½ teaspoons coriander seeds

½ teaspoon cumin seeds

½ cup packed dark brown sugar

½ cup cider vinegar

½ cup sherry vinegar

½ (3-ounce) can chipotles in adobo sauce

1 cup stadium-style mustard, such as Bertman Ballpark Mustard

I absolutely love barbecue. While it's popular throughout the Midwest, for some reason it doesn't have a huge presence in Cleveland. Maybe that's because what is around uses mostly sweet tomato-based sauces. Personally, I prefer the mustard-based sauces from South Carolina. One of my goals is to elevate C-Town barbecue to the next level, and this sauce is going to help me do it! Made with Bertman Ballpark Mustard—a Cleveland classic—this is now my favorite barbecue sauce. I'm hoping it will be yours, too.

1 In a nonreactive 2-quart saucepan set over medium-low heat, heat the olive oil, onion, garlic, and a good pinch of salt. Cook until the onion is translucent, about 2 minutes. Add the coriander and cumin and cook for 1 minute.

2 Add the brown sugar and cook for about 2 minutes, until it melts. Add the vinegars, increase the heat to medium-high, and boil for about 10 minutes, until reduced by one-quarter. Remove from the heat.

3 Puree the chipotle and adobo sauce in a blender or food processor until smooth. Stir the chipotle puree and mustard into the barbecue sauce. Let cool. Store covered in the refrigerator for up to 3 weeks.

SLOW-ROASTED PORK BELLY BUNS WITH CILANTRO & JALAPEÑO

Pork belly is such a magical cut of meat. Not only is it great when smoked for bacon and cured for pancetta, but it's also wonderful braised in hearty pork dishes. Here I roast it, which gives the skin a great crust, making it perfect for sandwiches. I like to top the meat with a healthy amount of cilantro and a good squeeze of lime to cut through the richness of the belly. If you like things a little spicy, don't be afraid to pile on the sliced jalapeño.

PORK BELLY

4 pounds skin-on pork belly (have your butcher cut it about 8 inches wide from the thickest part of the belly)

2 tablespoons grated fresh ginger

2 tablespoons coriander seeds, toasted and ground

1 tablespoon cumin seeds, toasted and ground

1 tablespoon kosher salt

1 teaspoon sugar

1 large red onion, quartered

1 cup roughly chopped peeled carrot

1 bay leaf, fresh or dried

1 bunch fresh thyme

BUNS

8 hot dog buns, split and toasted

Kosher salt

2 limes

1 bunch fresh cilantro

1 jalapeño, cut into thin rings

1 To cook the pork belly: Put the belly skin-side-up on a large cutting board. Using the tip of a sharp chef's knife, score the skin every 2 inches in a cross pattern. Combine the ginger, coriander, cumin, salt, and sugar. Rub both sides of the pork belly with this mixture, put the belly on a large plate skin-side-up, and refrigerate, uncovered, overnight.

2 Preheat the oven to 375°F.

3 Remove the belly from the fridge, rinse under cold water, and pat dry. Put it skin-side-up in a roasting pan and surround with the onion, carrots, bay leaf, and thyme. Pour water into the pan until it hits about one-third of the way up the sides of the pork belly. Cover the pan with foil and braise the pork belly until tender, about 2 hours.

4 Remove the foil. Increase the oven temperature to 400°F, and cook the belly for 1 hour, or until it reaches an internal temperature of 170°F and the skin is good and crispy. Remove from the pan to a cutting board and let cool slightly. Discard the vegetables.

5 Cut the pork belly into ¾-inch-thick slices and pile onto the hot dog buns. Sprinkle a little salt on the belly slices. Top each sandwich with a good squeeze of lime, a handful of fresh cilantro, and as many jalapeño rings as you see fit. Have plenty of napkins on hand!

ARANCINI

Arancini, essentially crispy fried rice balls, are a classic Roman street food. Served with warm tomato sauce for dipping, they are also one of my all-time favorite snacks. The rice balls I remember most as a kid were much larger than the ones I prepare today. Personally, I think they work better as just a two-bite treat. This recipe is a great way to use up any leftover risotto. Me, when I cook risotto, I make a double batch so I'm sure to have enough for *arancini!*

1 tablespoon olive oil

4 ounces sweet Italian sausage, homemade (page 87) or store-bought, removed from its casing (½ cup)

1 cup minced red onion

Kosher salt

1 cup Arborio or Carnaroli rice

3 cups chicken broth, preferably homemade (page 163), warmed

1 large egg

1 large egg yolk

1 cup freshly grated Parmesan cheese

8 ounces fresh mozzarella, cut into ¼-inch cubes

Canola oil, for deep-frying

1 cup plain, dried bread crumbs

1 Heat the olive oil in a 4-quart saucepan over medium-high heat. Break the sausage into small pieces, add to the pan, and brown on all sides, about 10 minutes. Add the onion along with ½ teaspoon salt and cook for 2 minutes. Add the rice, and toast, stirring with a wooden spoon, for 1 minute.

2 Reduce the heat to medium and add the chicken broth, ½ cup at a time, stirring constantly so the rice releases its starch. Continue to add the broth until the rice is tender and the risotto is creamy. This should take about 15 minutes. When the rice is cooked through, pour the mixture into a bowl and put in the refrigerator to cool.

3 Remove the rice from the refrigerator and add the egg, egg yolk, Parmesan, and ½ teaspoon salt. It is easiest to form the *arancini* with damp hands, so keep a small bowl of water nearby. With damp hands, form balls of about 2 tablespoons of the rice mixture each. With your thumb, make an indentation in the center and put about 1 teaspoon of the diced mozzarella in the center. Close up the indentation by re-forming the rice around the mozzarella to keep the cheese inside. You should get about 16 *arancini.* Store in the refrigerator until ready to cook, or for up to 1 day.

4 Heat 6 inches of oil in a pot or deep-fryer to 350°F. Meanwhile, coat the *arancini* in the bread crumbs, shaking off any excess. You want to bread these immediately before frying them so they don't get tacky and gummy. Deep-fry the *arancini* for 2½ minutes, or until very golden brown. Remove from the pot and lightly season with salt. Serve immediately.

ORECCHIETTE WITH CHORIZO & SWISS CHARD

This is a hearty pasta dish that packs a ton of savory flavor. It is quick, zesty, and perfect for the cool-weather months. The orecchiette shape, like a little ear the size of a teaspoon, catches bits of the chorizo and chard, making every bite delicious.

Kosher salt

1 pound dried orecchiette pasta

1 pound fresh chorizo sausage, homemade (page 91) or store-bought, removed from casing

1 pound Swiss chard, with stems, roughly chopped

1 cup cooked or drained canned cannellini beans

Grated zest and juice of 1 lemon

½ cup freshly grated Parmesan cheese

½ cup chopped fresh flat-leaf parsley

2 tablespoons unsalted butter

1 tablespoon extra-virgin olive oil

1 In a very large pot, bring 5 quarts water and 3 tablespoons salt to a boil. Add the pasta and cook until just al dente, about 1 minute less than package directions. Scoop out and reserve ¼ cup of the pasta water before draining the pasta. Do not rinse the pasta under water, as it will wash away the starch.

2 Meanwhile, heat a large Dutch oven over medium-high heat. Add the chorizo and cook, stirring occasionally, until browned, about 10 minutes. Add the Swiss chard and cook for 2 minutes, or until wilted. Add the beans, pasta, and the reserved pasta water simmer until the pasta is fully cooked, about 2 minutes.

3 Remove the pot from the heat, stir in the lemon zest and juice, the cheese, parsley, butter, and olive oil, and serve.

BUCATINI WITH BACON, TOMATOES & JALAPEÑO

I absolutely love pasta, and this is one of my all-time favorite dishes. Not only is it delicious, but it's super quick to make. You can get it on the dinner table in 10 minutes or so. Bucatini are like extra-thick spaghetti with a teeny hole that runs down the center of the strand. They're extra chewy and partner well with hearty ingredients like bacon, garlic, and jalapeño, though if you don't like spicy food, this recipe is still great without the jalapeño pepper.

Kosher salt

1 pound bucatini pasta

1 pound bacon, homemade (page 75) or store-bought slab, cut into large dice

4 garlic cloves, thinly sliced

1 large jalapeño, seeds and ribs removed, minced

2 cups whole peeled San Marzano tomatoes, chopped

1 cup chopped fresh flat-leaf parsley

2 tablespoons unsalted butter

½ cup freshly grated Parmesan cheese

1 In a very large pot, bring 5 quarts water and 3 tablespoons salt to a boil. Add the pasta and cook until just al dente, about 1 minute less than package directions. Scoop out and reserve ¼ cup of the pasta water before draining the pasta.

2 Meanwhile, put a large Dutch oven over medium-high heat. Add the bacon and cook until crisp, about 10 minutes. Don't drain off the bacon fat. Add the garlic and jalapeño to the pot and cook for 2 minutes.

3 Reduce the heat under the pot to medium-low. Add the tomatoes, bring to a simmer, and cook for 5 minutes. Add the pasta and reserved pasta water and simmer until the pasta is fully cooked, about 5 minutes.

4 Remove from the heat and add the parsley, butter, and Parmesan. Stir well and serve immediately.

PORK & RICOTTA MEATBALLS

I know everybody says this about their mom, but my mother makes the most incredible meatballs. Really! They always come out as light as a feather, absolutely delicious, and utterly addictive. Nobody is able to eat just one. Here is my take on Mom's meatballs. Hope you like them as much as I do.

½ cup cubed day-old bread

¼ cup whole milk

1½ pounds medium-ground pork (20% fat)

½ cup ricotta cheese

1 garlic clove, minced

1 shallot, minced

2 tablespoons chopped fresh flat-leaf parsley

Grated zest of 1 lemon

½ teaspoon ground coriander

¼ teaspoon ground cinnamon

1 teaspoon kosher salt

2 tablespoons olive oil

½ cup torn fresh basil leaves

¼ cup freshly grated Parmesan cheese

1 In a medium bowl, soak the bread in the milk. After the bread has thoroughly absorbed the milk, remove it from the bowl, squeezing out any excess liquid with your hands.

2 In a large bowl, combine the pork, soaked bread, ricotta, garlic, shallot, parsley, lemon zest, coriander, cinnamon, and salt. Mix with your hands to combine. Form into meatballs using ⅓ cup of the mixture for each one. It is easiest to form meatballs with slightly damp hands. You should have about 12 to 15 meatballs.

3 In a large frying pan, heat the olive oil over medium-high heat. Cook the meatballs for 2 to 3 minutes per side, until golden brown and cooked through. Remove to a large bowl, garnish with the basil leaves, and top with the Parmesan cheese.

MUSSELS WITH CHORIZO

Liz and I have never managed to eat at a French brasserie without her ordering a platter of mussels. It is an absolute given. And over the many years we've been together, we have tasted a million different variations. We have also cooked what seems like a million versions: This one is our personal favorite. Add some crispy French fries or crusty bread, some rich, creamy aioli, and a cold Belgian beer and you have the ideal late lunch or early dinner.

2 pounds mussels, cleaned

2 tablespoons olive oil

8 ounces fresh chorizo, homemade (page 91) or store-bought, removed from casing (1½ cups)

1 cup Chardonnay

1 cup chicken broth, preferably homemade (page 163)

2 tablespoons unsalted butter

¾ teaspoon kosher salt

½ cup chopped fresh flat-leaf parsley

1 Rinse the mussels under cold water and remove any beards.

2 In a large enameled Dutch oven, heat the olive oil over medium-high heat. When the oil is hot, add the chorizo in large pieces and brown on all sides, about 10 minutes. Using a slotted spoon, remove the chorizo to a plate.

3 Raise the heat under the pot to high, add the mussels and Chardonnay, and immediately cover the pot. Cook for about 3 minutes, or until the mussels have opened. With a slotted spoon, move the mussels to large serving bowls, discarding any that do not open.

4 To the same pot, add the chicken broth and bring to a boil. Whisk in the butter and salt. Reduce the heat to medium and add the chorizo and parsley. Pour this mixture directly over the mussels and serve immediately with spoons. You don't want to waste any of that flavorful broth!

GROUND LAMB

LEG OF GOAT (BONE-IN)

LAMB & GOAT

LAMB
SPARE RIBS

FRENCHED
RACK OF LAMB

LAMB NECK

Lamb and goat might not compete with pork and beef in the popularity department, but when it comes to flavor, I think they are right at the top. Having a mother who is part Greek, I ate more than my fair share of lamb and goat growing up. To this day, they still are two of my favorite meats to cook with and eat. The good news is that unlike beef, pork, and poultry, which very often come from factory farms, lambs and goats almost always are allowed to graze freely on pastures rather than cramped in feedlots.

HOW TO CHOOSE LAMB & GOAT

When it comes to lamb, the biggest decision you'll have to make is choosing between domestic, Australian, and New Zealand. Due to regulations where it is raised, New Zealand and Australian lamb is almost always free-range and antibiotic- and hormone-free, all of which are great features. What I don't love about lamb from those places, however, is the fact that it's too small and too mild in flavor. In fact, I often refer to the meat as lamb for beginners, owing to its mild flavor in comparison to domestic lamb. (My advice for people who don't like any sort of gamy flavor whatsoever is to skip lamb and goat altogether and just buy beef; it's cheaper!) I say: If you're going to eat lamb, the meat should taste like lamb! That's why I prefer domestic lamb, which is often nearly twice the size of its foreign counterparts, meaning more fat and more flavor. Domestic lamb is more expensive than either New Zealand or

Australian lamb, but it's a price I'm willing to pay.

As with any food, buy from somebody you trust, ask a lot of questions, and understand the labels and terminology. Seek out only domestic lamb from producers that use no growth hormones or antibiotics. Most American lamb is raised in Colorado, but my favorite producer is Jamison Farm in western Pennsylvania. Their lambs and sheep roam free and graze on an all-natural diet without access to herbicides or insecticides and are not given hormones or antibiotics. And by allowing the lamb to age a bit after the slaughter, Jamison produces a more tender, more flavorful meat.

Once you have conquered any fear of lamb, go for goat. I find the flavor slightly sweeter than that of lamb, but still with a nice gaminess to it. Most of the so-called lamb roasts I attended as a kid were actually goat roasts, because the meat was much less expensive, but just as tasty. I might go so far as to say that I think goat tastes even better than lamb. A great way to ease your way into goat is with a pasta sauce, like Goat Ragù (page 137), which I often pair with Fresh Pappardelle (page 246).

Another benefit to cooking with lamb and goat is their size. Both are hundreds of pounds lighter than any pig or cow, meaning that chefs and home cooks often can have access to the whole beast. This is as eco-nomical, resourceful, and sustainable as you can get. So, be adventurous. If you happen to be a fan of braised beef short ribs, you should definitely give Braised Lamb Necks (page 127) a try. I promise it'll be one of the most flavorful braises you've ever had. Maybe you can work your way up to a full-fledged lamb (or goat) roast.

COOK IT RIGHT: LAMB & GOAT

Lamb and goat have unique flavors—which people either like or not. I, of course, love them both especially for their slightly gamy flavor. Although I find all cuts from these animals worthwhile, my favorite preparations include chops fresh off the charcoal grill and slow-braised shanks.

GRILL/PAN-ROAST/BROIL

» Rib chops
» Rack
» Shoulder chops
» Loin chops
» Liver
» Kidneys

BRAISE

» Shank
» Belly/breast
» Head
» Shoulder chops

OVEN-ROAST

» Rack
» Leg
» Shoulder
» Saddle

SMOKE

» Butt (shoulder)
» Leg (ham)
» Belly
» Shank
» Rack
» Cheeks
» Ribs

GRIND

» Shoulder
» Belly/breast

STEW

» Shoulder chops
» Belly/breast
» Shank

SPICY LAMB & MINT SAUSAGE

The key to making great lamb sausage is to remove all the fat and sinew from the meat before grinding, and substituting pork fat in its place. It makes for a creamier sausage with a cleaner, less gamy flavor. This recipe is quite spicy, the way I like it. If you aren't a fan of heat, go ahead and reduce the amount of chipotle, or eliminate it altogether. I try and make this sausage toward the end of spring, when the lamb is beautiful, the mint is thriving, and it's just hot enough outside so the chipotle makes you sweat. I like to grill the lamb sausages and serve on hot dog buns topped with crumbled feta and roasted peppers.

3 pounds lamb shoulder, fat and sinew removed, cubed

1 pound fatback, cut into 1-inch cubes

1 (2-ounce) can chipotles in adobo sauce, pureed with sauce

1 cup chopped fresh mint

¼ cup chopped fresh chives

Grated zest of 2 oranges

3 tablespoons kosher salt

1 tablespoon freshly ground black pepper

½ cup whole milk, chilled

½ cup dry red wine, chilled

6 feet of hog casing, soaked overnight and rinsed (see page 35), optional

1 Combine the lamb, fatback, pureed chipotles, mint, chives, orange zest, salt, and pepper in a gallon-sized zip-top bag and refrigerate overnight.

2 Thoroughly chill all the sausage-grinding equipment, the mixing bowl, and the paddle attachment. Grind the marinated lamb mixture through the medium-sized die into the chilled bowl. Add the milk and red wine and blend with the paddle attachment until well incorporated. Keep refrigerated until ready to use or for up to 5 days.

3 Stuff the filling into a hog casing (see page 36) and grill until the sausage reaches an internal temperature of 160°F; form into patties and pan-roast until browned and cooked through; or leave it loose to use in steamed mussels or clams in broth, or with scrambled eggs.

LAMB BURGER WITH ARUGULA, FETA & CUCUMBERS

This fun and tasty burger is an obvious nod to my Greek heritage. What really makes this burger pop, in my opinion, is the crunchy cucumber topping with a nice squeeze of lemon.

5 pounds ground lamb (ask your butcher for a mix of two-thirds shoulder and one-third belly)

1 tablespoon coriander seeds, toasted and ground

¼ cup chopped fresh mint

Grated zest and juice of 2 lemons

Kosher salt

1½ cups crumbled feta

10 hamburger buns, split

1 English cucumber, sliced

2 cups arugula

1 Mix the lamb with the coriander, mint, and the lemon zest. Form the meat into 10 patties, making sure you don't compress the patties too tightly. Try to make the patties slightly wider than the buns, since they'll shrink a bit when they cook.

2 Heat a charcoal or gas grill to medium-high.

3 Season the patties liberally with salt and put on the grill. Cook for 4 to 5 minutes per side, depending on your temperature preference. I love these burgers somewhere between medium-rare and medium. When the burgers are almost done, put some feta on each patty to melt while you also toast the buns on the grill.

4 Put one burger on each of the bottom buns and top with cucumber, arugula, and a nice squeeze of lemon juice.

ROASTED RACK OF LAMB

I prefer to cook rack of lamb low and slow rather than hot and fast. While this might sound counterintuitive, it produces great results. This method eliminates that annoying bullet in the middle—the blood-rare center surrounded by gray, well-done meat—replacing it with evenly cooked meat throughout. The longer roasting time also allows the lamb fat to melt slowly and baste the meat. I think you'll love this recipe; it's extremely forgiving and practically foolproof. Serve with Skordalia (page 239) and Orange Salad (page 212).

Grated zest of 2 lemons

2 tablespoons chopped
fresh rosemary

¼ cup kosher salt

Pinch of sugar

2 (8-bone) racks of lamb,
chine bone removed,
Frenched

¼ cup canola oil

1 Mix together the lemon zest, rosemary, salt, and sugar. Season the racks on all sides with this mixture, cover, and put in the refrigerator overnight. This acts like a quick cure, which will add flavor to the lamb when it is cooked.

2 Preheat the oven to 300°F.

3 Put a large sauté pan over medium heat and add the oil. Put one of the seasoned racks in the pan fat-side-down, and sear until golden brown, 3 to 5 minutes. Flip the rack and sear the other side for a few minutes. Remove to a rimmed baking sheet fat-side-up, and repeat the browning process with the other rack.

4 Put the baking sheet with both racks on it in the oven and roast until the meat registers 120° to 125°F in the center, 20 to 25 minutes. Let rest for 5 minutes before cutting into chops and serving.

GRILLED LAMB LIVERS WITH GREEK YOGURT, MINT & ALMONDS

Admittedly, I am a lover of liver (especially with a nice bottle of Chianti!). But of all the varieties of liver out there, lamb might just be my favorite. As with lamb meat, the liver has a mild muskiness to it that I think makes it taste special. With this and most grilled liver recipes, you want to cook the meat very quickly and not go past medium-rare. Make sure all your garnishes are prepped before you begin cooking.

1 cup Greek yogurt

Grated zest and juice of 1 orange

3 pounds cleaned lamb livers

Kosher salt and freshly ground black pepper

2 tablespoons olive oil

1 cup fresh mint leaves, torn

½ cup thinly sliced breakfast radishes

½ cup Marcona almonds, toasted and chopped

4 tablespoons extra-virgin olive oil

1 Whisk together the yogurt and orange zest and juice. Keep refrigerated.

2 Season the livers with salt and pepper, 2 tablespoons olive oil, and 2 tablespoons of the yogurt mix. Put in a gallon-sized zip-top bag to marinate in the fridge for 2 to 3 hours.

3 Heat a charcoal or gas grill to medium-high.

4 Remove the livers from the bag and season with salt and pepper. Grill for 2 minutes per side, or until medium-rare. If you have a thicker piece of liver, it may take as long as 3 to 4 minutes per side. Transfer the livers to a serving platter.

5 In a bowl, toss together the mint, radishes, almonds, and 2 tablespoons of the extra-virgin olive oil. Serve the liver topped with a nice dollop of the yogurt mix, the mint salad, and the remaining 2 tablespoons extra-virgin olive oil.

GRILLED LAMB CHOPS WITH LAVENDER SALT

The first time I tried this simple but brilliant pairing was at a Share Our Strength fund-raiser in Toledo. At the dinner for chefs and sponsors the night before the main event, Labib Hajjar, who runs my favorite Middle Eastern restaurant, The Beirut, was manning the grills. To prepare his dish, he took beautiful domestic lamb chops, brushed them with olive oil, and grilled them to medium-rare. When cooked, the chops were sprinkled with lavender-infused sea salt and handed out like lollipops to hungry guests. Like many of the best recipes, this one is easy but unforgettable. If you want to make extra lavender salt to save, go ahead; it keeps well. Also, if you prefer rosemary, thyme, or Greek oregano, feel free to substitute one of those herbs (though lavender is my favorite).

2 tablespoons dried lavender

½ cup flaky sea salt, such as Cyprus Flake or Maldon

24 domestic lamb chops

Olive oil

1 Rub the dried lavender between your fingers to release the oils. Add it to the salt and mix to combine.

2 Allow the chops to come to room temperature for 20 to 30 minutes before grilling. Heat a charcoal or gas grill to medium-high.

3 Brush the chops with olive oil and put on the grill. Cook until medium-rare, 2 to 3 minutes per side. When done, remove the chops from the grill, sprinkle both sides with the lavender salt, and pass to appreciative family and friends.

CRISPY LAMB SWEETBREADS, SICILIAN-STYLE

If you are looking to try your hand at preparing offal, this is a great recipe to start with. The flavors are addictive: bright, briny, and a touch sweet, all at once. Despite the overall length of time required (you have to start this recipe two days in advance of serving), it is actually relatively easy to pull off. And once the sweetbreads are poached and cleaned, the rest of the dish can be prepared in a single pan, which is always a bonus in my book. Apart from the sweetbreads, most of the ingredients are probably already in your pantry.

SWEETBREADS

2 pounds lamb sweetbreads

Kosher salt

1 cup diced celery

1 large red onion, quartered

1 cup diced leeks, white parts only

1 lemon, halved

1 teaspoon black peppercorns

1 bay leaf, fresh or dried

3 tablespoons unsalted butter

Rice flour, for dredging

2 tablespoons pine nuts

1 cup halved red grapes

2 tablespoons salted capers, rinsed

1 anchovy, minced

1 shallot, minced

¼ cup Marsala wine

Grated zest and juice of 1 orange

3 tablespoons chopped fresh flat-leaf parsley

1 To poach the sweetbreads: Two nights before cooking the main recipe, submerge the sweetbreads in salted ice water and refrigerate overnight. This begins the cleaning process, drawing out any impurities that may be left in the meat.

2 The following day, put a large pot over medium-high heat. Add 4 quarts water, ¼ cup salt, the celery, onion, leeks, lemon, peppercorns, and bay leaf and bring to a simmer. The poaching liquid should taste very salty at this point.

3 Meanwhile, remove the sweetbreads from their soaking liquid, drain, and put in a large bowl. Add 8 cups ice to the bowl. When the poaching liquid reaches a simmer, add the sweetbreads and ice and stir. The ice acts as a buffer that prevents the sweetbreads from cooking too quickly. The goal is to poach them slowly, so they end up evenly cooked and creamy throughout. Lower the heat to medium-low and poach, stirring occasionally, for about 17 minutes. When done, the sweetbreads will turn pale white and feel somewhat firm. Remove from the poaching liquid and plunge into an ice bath. Discard the poaching liquid.

4 When the sweetbreads are cool, drain them, and remove the thin membrane that covers the whole organ. It should peel off easily using just your fingers. When it is off, look for any pieces of solidified fat and remove them. You may have to break up the sweetbreads slightly to do so. When fully cleaned, arrange the sweetbreads in a single layer on a kitchen-towel-lined baking sheet. Put another towel on top, followed by another baking sheet. Put a few heavy plates on top to evenly weight down the sweetbreads. Put in the refrigerator overnight.

5 In a large sauté pan over medium-high heat, melt the butter. Meanwhile, season the sweetbreads with salt and dredge with rice flour, shaking off any excess. Sear the sweetbreads in the butter until golden brown, about 2 minutes per side. Be careful not to crowd the pan. When browned, remove the sweetbreads from the pan to warm serving plates, leaving any butter behind in the pan.

6 Reduce the heat under the pan to medium and toast the pine nuts. When the pine nuts are toasted and the butter browned, about 1 minute, add the grapes, capers, anchovy, and shallot. Add a pinch of salt and cook for 1 minute. Add the Marsala and orange zest and juice. When this comes to a simmer, taste and adjust for seasoning. Stir in the parsley.

7 Spoon the pan sauce over the sweetbreads, and serve immediately.

SMOKED LAMB RIBS ON THE GRILL WITH LEMON, OREGANO & HONEY

If you don't own a smoker, this is a great way to do ribs on the grill. I first saw this technique used by Adam Perry Lang, who is not only a great barbecue chef but also a great all-around chef. In fact, he knows more about meat than practically anybody I've met. For this recipe I use lamb spareribs, but the technique works just as well with pork ribs too, though cook times will vary. Feel free to substitute your favorite barbecue sauce for the glaze.

RIBS

3 tablespoons dried oregano

3 tablespoons garlic salt

2 tablespoons smoked paprika

2 tablespoons coriander seeds, toasted and ground

1 tablespoon freshly ground black pepper

1 teaspoon kosher salt

6 racks lamb spareribs

Juice of 2 lemons

GLAZE

3 tablespoons honey

¼ cup red wine vinegar

2 garlic cloves, minced

1 cup minced red onion

3 lemons

Flaky sea salt, such as Cyprus Flake or Maldon, for serving

3 tablespoons fresh oregano leaves

3 tablespoons extra-virgin olive oil

1 To prepare the ribs: Mix together the dried oregano, garlic salt, paprika, coriander, pepper, and kosher salt. Moisten the ribs with the lemon juice and then coat all sides with the rub, making sure to distribute it evenly.

2 Set up your grill or smoker for indirect heat, meaning the ribs will not be directly over the heat source. Using low heat and apple-wood chips, put the ribs on the cool part of the grill, cover, and smoke for 1 hour.

3 Meanwhile, whisk together the glaze ingredients.

4 Arrange 2 of the lamb racks on a large piece of foil, overlapping them like roof shingles. Pour one-third of the glaze on top of the ribs and seal tightly in the foil, being careful not to tear it. Wrap in a second sheet of foil. Repeat twice, using the remaining racks and glaze.

5 Return the ribs to the grill and cook meat-side-down for 30 minutes over low heat. Flip the foil bundles and continue cooking for 30 minutes. Remove the ribs from the grill and let rest in the foil for 30 minutes.

6 Meanwhile, increase the grill heat to medium-high. Cut the lemons in half and grill flesh-side-down until nicely marked and slightly soft, 3 to 5 minutes.

7 Remove the ribs from the foil, put on the hot grill meat-side-down, and cook for 4 minutes. Flip and cook for 2 minutes. Remove the ribs from the grill and garnish with the grilled lemons, sea salt, fresh oregano, and extra-virgin olive oil.

BRAISED LAMB NECKS

I know what some of you are thinking: Why the hell would anybody want to eat a lamb neck?! Well, if you are a fan of short ribs or osso buco, then you will love this dish. Not only do lamb necks cost half as much as those cuts, but they pack every bit as much flavor. This is a long, slow braise that needs to cook in the oven for about 4 hours. Garnish with Grapefruit Salad (page 214).

6 pounds lamb necks

Kosher salt and freshly ground black pepper

2 tablespoons olive oil, or more if needed

2 celery stalks, roughly chopped

1 cup roughly chopped peeled carrot

1 cup roughly chopped red onion

1 Fresno chile, halved

½ cup tomato paste

Small bundle of fresh thyme

1 bay leaf

1 head garlic, cloves separated, smashed, and peeled

2 cups dry red wine

⅓ cup red wine vinegar

3 quarts chicken broth, preferably homemade (page 163)

1 Season the lamb necks with salt and pepper, cover, and refrigerate overnight. Remove from the refrigerator 30 minutes before cooking.

2 Preheat the oven to 325°F.

3 In a large Dutch oven over medium-high, heat the olive oil. Working in batches, brown the lamb necks, cooking for a few minutes on all sides. Transfer the necks to a plate as they are finished browning.

4 Pour off all but 2 or 3 tablespoons fat from the pot. Add the celery, carrots, onion, and chile, along with a large pinch of salt. Cook over medium heat until the vegetables are softened, about 7 minutes. Add the tomato paste and cook, stirring, until the mixture is glossy, about 2 minutes. Add the thyme, bay leaf, and garlic and cook for 2 minutes. Deglaze the pot with the wine and vinegar and simmer to reduce by half. Add the chicken broth and bring the liquid to a simmer. Taste and adjust for seasoning.

5 Return the lamb necks to the pot, cover, and braise in the oven until the meat is tender, about 4 hours. Move the necks from the braising pot to a clean pot. Strain the braising liquid over the necks, discarding the solids. If you have time, let cool and refrigerate overnight. Discard the fat from the top before reheating.

6 To serve, reheat the necks in the liquid. Put the necks on a platter and spoon some sauce on top.

LEG OF LAMB SOUVLAKI

I love cooking souvlaki on the grill in summer, and while it can be made with just about any meat, I think leg of lamb is the best. I usually eat the meat right off the skewer, but it's also great served in a warm pita. When grilling the lamb, start it on the hotter side of the grill and then move it over lower heat to cook slowly until it reaches medium or even medium-well. I know most chefs prefer lamb on the rare side, but in this case, the additional time really helps tenderize the meat. Don't worry; the marinade will keep it juicy. Serve this with Honey Nectarines (page 210).

2 shallots, minced

2 garlic cloves, minced

1 jalapeño, seeded and minced

2 tablespoons chopped fresh oregano

Juice of 1 lemon

½ cup extra-virgin olive oil

2 pounds boneless leg of lamb, trimmed and cut into 1½- to 2-inch chunks

1 cup Greek yogurt

1 Combine the shallots, garlic, jalapeño, oregano, lemon juice, and olive oil in a gallon-sized zip-top bag. Add the lamb, turning to coat, and refrigerate for at least 3 hours, but preferably overnight.

2 If using wooden skewers, soak 12 to 16 of them in water for at least 20 minutes. Heat a charcoal or gas grill or grill pan to medium-high.

3 Remove the lamb from the marinade and thread 2 pieces onto one end of each skewer. Grill over high heat for 2 minutes per side, then move to the cooler part of the grill. Cover the grill and cook until the meat reaches an internal temperature of 145°F, 4 to 5 minutes.

4 Serve the souvlaki with a dollop of Greek yogurt.

MOUSSAKA

Moussaka is the ultimate Greek comfort food, and it was one of my favorite dishes growing up. This is basically the version my mother made, with only a few minor tweaks (don't tell her). It is just as good to eat the second day as it is the day it's made, so don't worry about leftovers.

LAMB

1 cup red wine

¼ cup golden raisins

4 tablespoons extra-virgin olive oil

1 pound ground lamb

½ teaspoon red pepper flakes

½ teaspoon ground cinnamon

½ teaspoon ground coriander

¼ teaspoon ground cumin

Kosher salt and freshly ground black pepper

1 large yellow onion, halved and thinly sliced

1 red bell pepper, stemmed, cored, and thinly sliced

5 garlic cloves, finely chopped

2 tablespoons tomato paste

1 (28-ounce) can plum tomatoes, pureed with juice until smooth

¼ cup chopped fresh flat-leaf parsley, plus more for serving

¼ cup chopped fresh mint

2 tablespoons chopped fresh oregano

EGGPLANT

1½ cups canola oil

1½ pounds eggplant, cut crosswise into ½-inch-thick slices

Kosher salt and freshly ground black pepper

1 To cook the lamb: Heat the wine until warm to the touch. Soak the raisins in the wine for 30 minutes. Drain, reserving the wine and raisins separately.

2 Meanwhile, in a 6-quart saucepan, heat 1 tablespoon of the olive oil over high heat. Add the lamb, red pepper flakes, cinnamon, coriander, and cumin, season with salt and black pepper, and cook, stirring to break up the meat, until browned, about 5 minutes. Remove the lamb with a slotted spoon and set aside. Discard any accumulated liquid in the pan.

3 Return the pan to the heat, add the remaining 3 tablespoons olive oil, and heat until it begins to shimmer. Add the onion and bell pepper and cook for 5 minutes, or until soft. Add the garlic and cook for 1 minute. Add the tomato paste and cook for 1 minute.

4 Return the lamb to the pan, add the reserved wine, and cook, stirring occasionally, for 5 minutes, or until the liquid is almost completely evaporated. Add the tomato puree and the soaked raisins and bring to a boil. Reduce the heat to medium-low and simmer for 30 minutes, or until thickened. Stir in the ¼ cup parsley, the mint, and oregano and taste and adjust the seasoning with salt and black pepper as needed. Remove from the heat.

5 To cook the eggplant: In a 12-inch skillet, heat the canola oil over medium-high heat. Season the eggplant slices on both sides with salt and pepper. Working in batches, fry the eggplant slices for about 2 minutes on each side, until tender and lightly golden brown. When done, transfer to paper towels to drain.

(RECIPE CONTINUES)

BÉCHAMEL

6 tablespoons unsalted butter, plus more for the dish

½ cup all-purpose flour

2½ cups whole milk

1 bay leaf, fresh or dried

Kosher salt and freshly ground black pepper

⅛ teaspoon freshly grated nutmeg

3 large egg yolks

1 cup Greek yogurt

Grated zest of 1 lemon

½ cup crumbled feta

6 Preheat the oven to 400°F.

7 To make the béchamel: In a medium saucepan over medium heat, melt the 6 tablespoons butter. Add the flour and cook, whisking constantly, for about 2 minutes, until pale and smooth. Whisk in the milk and bay leaf and cook, whisking, until thickened, about 30 minutes. Discard the bay leaf and season the sauce with salt, pepper, and the nutmeg. Set aside to cool for 5 minutes.

8 In a small bowl, whisk together the egg yolks, yogurt, and lemon zest. Whisk into the béchamel sauce until smooth. Whisk in the feta.

9 Butter a 3-quart baking dish. Arrange half of the eggplant slices on the bottom of the dish. Cover with half of the lamb mixture. Arrange the remaining eggplant slices on top of the lamb, and top with remaining lamb mixture. Evenly spread the béchamel over the top. Put the dish on a baking sheet and bake for 45 to 50 minutes, until browned and bubbly.

10 Let cool for at least 20 minutes before serving, garnished with chopped parsley, if desired.

BRAISED GOAT TACOS

Although this dish is relatively easy to make, it does require some planning ahead to marinate and braise the goat. But once the goat is braised, it keeps really well in the fridge for a couple of days and reheats perfectly. If you want to go all out, prepare homemade Corn Tortillas (page 249), made with lard, naturally. If you're not in the mood to whip up your own, grab some fresh tortillas from the Mexican grocery.

1 cup sherry vinegar

1 cup olive oil

10 garlic cloves, smashed and peeled

1 cinnamon stick

1 tablespoon cumin seeds, toasted

1 tablespoon coriander seeds, toasted

2 teaspoons ancho chile powder

¼ teaspoon red pepper flakes

2 tablespoons packed light brown sugar

1 (5-pound) bone-in leg of goat (ask your butcher to cut it into 5 or 6 sections)

3 tablespoons canola oil

2 (12-ounce) bottles of your favorite Mexican beer

1 (16-ounce) can crushed tomatoes, with juice

12 (6-inch) corn tortillas, homemade (page 249) or store-bought, warmed

Sliced radishes, fresh cilantro sprigs, and lime wedges, for serving

1 In a mixing bowl, whisk together the vinegar, olive oil, garlic, cinnamon, cumin, coriander, ancho powder, red pepper flakes, and brown sugar. Put the goat in a large zip-top bag, add the marinade, and refrigerate overnight or for up to 2 days.

2 Preheat the oven to 350°F.

3 Remove the meat from the marinade and pat it dry. Reserve the liquid. Put a large Dutch oven over medium-high heat and add the canola oil. Brown the goat for 3 to 4 minutes per side. Add the reserved marinade, the beer, and tomatoes to the pot and bring to a simmer. Cover, transfer to the oven, and braise until the meat is falling off the bone, 2 to 3 hours.

4 Remove from the oven and let the meat cool in the juices. When cool enough to handle, pull the meat off the bones and set the meat aside, discarding the bones and fat. Strain the liquid into a smaller saucepan over low heat, discarding any solids. Shred the meat with two forks or your fingers. Put the shredded meat in a bowl, top with the warm sauce, and toss to coat.

5 Serve with corn tortillas and sliced radishes, fresh cilantro sprigs, and lime wedges for garnish.

LAMB BOLOGNESE WITH CAVATELLI

For such a satisfying comfort food, Bolognese is a remarkably straightforward sauce to make. Whenever possible, try and make the sauce the day ahead, which gives the flavors a chance to really meld together. If I find myself with a huge cache of great lamb, I'll make a double batch of this sauce and freeze half of it for another night. While Bolognese is traditionally served with tagliatelle, for this recipe I like to pair the sauce with ricotta cavatelli, like we do at Lola. It's also great with gnocchi. The fresh mint at the end really brightens up the whole dish.

1 tablespoon olive oil

2 pounds ground lamb

Kosher salt

1 cup diced red onion

3 garlic cloves, minced

1 cup finely diced peeled carrot

1 cup finely diced celery

1 cup dry red wine

1 (28-ounce) can whole plum tomatoes, with juice

1 bay leaf, preferably fresh

6 sprigs fresh oregano

2 pounds fresh cavatelli

1 cup fresh mint, torn

½ cup freshly grated Parmesan cheese

2 tablespoons unsalted butter

1 Put a large saucepan over medium-high heat. Add the olive oil and lamb along with a large pinch of salt. Cook the lamb until browned, about 10 minutes. Remove from the pan and set aside.

2 Add the onion and garlic to the pan and cook for 3 minutes, until softened. Add the carrots and celery and cook for another 3 minutes. Deglaze the pan with the red wine, using a wooden spoon to scrape up the tasty bits on the bottom of the pan. Cook until nearly evaporated.

3 Return the lamb to the pan along with the tomatoes and their juice. Bring to a simmer, breaking up the tomatoes with a spoon. Add the bay leaf and oregano and taste and adjust for seasoning. Simmer for about 2 hours, skimming off any excess fat that collects on the top. Remove the bay leaf and oregano sprigs.

4 When the sauce is ready, bring a large pot of salted water to a boil. Drop the fresh cavatelli into the water and cook until they float, 1 to 2 minutes. Remove from the water with a slotted spoon and add to the sauce. If the sauce is too thick, add ¼ cup of the pasta water. Remove from the heat and stir in the mint, Parmesan, and butter. Serve immediately.

GOAT RAGÙ WITH PAPPARDELLE

Goat is one of the most widely consumed meats on the planet, but it has never really gained a huge following here in the States. That's too bad, because the meat is fantastic, possessing a mild sweetness that allows it to work well in so many recipes, this one included. Braising the meat in milk helps to tenderize it while giving the sauce more body. If you have the time, prepare this hearty *ragù* the day before and reheat it. It always tastes better on the second (or even third) day.

6 tablespoons olive oil

2 pounds bone-in goat shoulder

Kosher salt and freshly ground black pepper

6 cups whole milk

Small bundle of fresh thyme

1 bay leaf, fresh or dried

1 small cinnamon stick

1 cup finely diced red onion

1 cup finely diced peeled carrot

1 cup finely diced peeled celery root

2 cups crushed San Marzano tomatoes

2 tablespoons red pepper flakes

2 pounds fresh pappardelle, homemade (page 246) or store-bought

½ cup grated Graviera or Parmesan cheese

Freshly grated Parmesan cheese, for serving

1 Preheat the oven to 300°F.

2 Put an enameled cast-iron pot or Dutch oven over medium-high heat and add 3 tablespoons of the olive oil. Season the goat with salt and pepper and add it to the pot. Cook until browned on all sides, about 15 minutes. Add the milk, thyme, bay leaf, and cinnamon stick to the pot and bring to a boil. Cover with aluminum foil, put the lid on the pot, and transfer to the oven. Braise until the meat is tender enough to pull off the bone, about 4 hours.

3 Remove the meat from the pot and set aside to cool. Pull the meat from the bones in large pieces, reserving the meat and the bones separately. Strain the braising liquid. Measure ½ cup and reserve.

4 In the same pot, heat 1 tablespoon of the olive oil over low heat and add the onion, carrot, and celery root. Cook for 8 minutes. Add the tomatoes, reserved bones, red pepper flakes, and reserved ½ cup braising liquid. Bring to a simmer and cook for 30 minutes. Check and adjust the seasoning with salt and pepper as needed. Remove and discard the bones. Keep the *ragù* warm.

5 Bring a large pot of salted water to a boil. Drop in the pappardelle and cook until al dente, about 4 minutes. Remove the pasta from the water with a slotted spoon and add it to the sauce along with ¼ cup of the pasta water, depending on the thickness of the sauce. Gently stir the pasta into the sauce and remove it from the heat. Stir in the Graviera cheese and the remaining 2 tablespoons olive oil. Serve immediately topped with Parmesan.

CHICKEN NECKS

WHOLE CHICKEN

LIVERS

WHOLE WINGS

CHICKEN LEGS AND THIGHS

BONELESS TURKEY THIGH

POULTRY

SPLIT TURKEY BREAST (BONE-IN)

Everybody knows about my adoration for pork. And beef is pretty much synonymous with America. But here's a little secret: I go crazy for chicken, especially when it's my wife's amazing roasted chicken. (Food always tastes better when someone else does the cooking!) When it's done to perfection—mouthwateringly tender, juicy meat concealed beneath a crackling-crisp skin—a whole roasted bird transcends its humble barnyard beginnings. And here's another thing: Almost everybody else loves chicken, too, and for good reason—it is accessible, affordable, and quick to prepare, making it one of the most popular meats to cook at home.

HOW TO CHOOSE CHICKEN & TURKEY

Today's confusing—and misleading—food labels make it really hard to know what the heck we're buying half the time. That's especially true in the case of chicken. Labels like "natural" and "free-range" sound noble enough—I mean, what could be wrong with *natural?* The sad reality is that many of these labels mean next to nothing. We read the words "free-range" and we picture happy chickens pecking at worms and clover on a sun-dappled hill. Ha! To qualify for that label, producers need only to prove that the birds have *access* to the outside, which could be as little as a small door at one end of a football-field-sized barn. "Natural" isn't a whole lot better. It basically means that chicken can't be artificially flavored or pre-served with chemicals. But there is no ban on injecting the birds with broth or water to beef up their weight, for example.

As with most things in life, the best way to avoid all this nonsense is to shop from somebody you trust. I ask my purveyors and butchers questions, and so should you. Is this chicken raised only on a diet of organic feed? Did it have a little room to roam? Were any growth hormones or antibiotics given to the animal at any stage in its life? How old was the bird when it was slaughtered? (This last question lets me see if the bird is unnaturally large for its age, which should be at least 2 months old.) All of these facts are more important to me than what particular breed the chicken is.

Look for chicken that is creamy in color with a slight yellow tinge to the meat and skin. Chicken, like people, shouldn't look like it fell asleep in a tanning salon. The meat should be firm to the touch and never slimy. An unnaturally large breast and weak, skinny legs are a good sign that the chicken had no room to roam. Basically, avoid any chicken that looks like it could be a new cast member on *Jersey Shore* and you'll be fine.

The same basic rules apply to turkey as to chicken. That being said, I do have some personal preferences particular to turkey. Bigger isn't always better when it comes to turkey. I would much rather cook two 10-pound turkeys than one 20-pound beast. For starters, smaller turkeys are just easier to work with. Massive platters of hot, heavy food are recipes for disaster. I also think the smaller ones are juicier and more tender and flavorful than big, old "Toms." For families like mine that prefer just as much dark meat as white, heritage-breed turkeys are a better choice than domesticated birds with unnaturally gigantic breasts. The heritage breeds have a more equal balance of dark to white meat. (One exception I would make is when I'm smoking a breast, because heritage-breed turkey breasts are smaller.)

COOK IT RIGHT: CHICKEN, TURKEY & GAME BIRDS

There are not many pleasures in life better than a perfectly roasted whole chicken, which is why, of all the ways to cook poultry, it remains my favorite. If you are cooking through the cuts, remember that chicken is extremely lean, making only the thighs, necks, and backs suitable for long cooking techniques like braising and stewing. For game birds like quail, pheasant, and partridge—which tend to be small and lean—fast, hot cooking methods such as roasting and grilling work best. In other words, approach these birds as you would a chicken. In the case of duck and goose—both boasting thick layers of fat—longer and lower heat cooking methods work best, giving the fat time to render fully.

GRILL/PAN-ROAST/BROIL

» Breast
» Thighs
» Legs
» Livers
» Giblets

BRAISE

» Thighs
» Legs
» Backs
» Necks

OVEN-ROAST

» Whole

SMOKE

» Whole
» Breast
» Thighs
» Legs
» Necks

GRIND

» Thighs

STEW

» Thighs
» Backs
» Necks

CRISPY CHICKEN LIVERS WITH POLENTA, BACON & MUSHROOMS

This dish has been a staple at Lolita since the day we opened. It is comfort food at its peak, elevating humble polenta and chicken livers to epic levels. The polenta is easy to prepare, but it does require some time. Once it's finished, keep it warm on the stovetop while you prepare the chicken livers. A simple pan sauce is all it takes to finish this killer dish.

2 pounds chicken livers, cleaned

2 cups buttermilk

1 cup diced bacon

5 cups oyster mushrooms, broken up into small pieces

½ cup dry white wine

1 cup chicken broth, preferably homemade (page 163), warmed

2 tablespoons unsalted butter

2 tablespoons thinly sliced fresh flat-leaf parsley

Kosher salt and freshly ground black pepper

Canola oil

All-purpose flour, for dredging

Soft Polenta with Aged Cheddar (page 248)

1 Soak the chicken livers in the buttermilk in the refrigerator for at least 3 hours or overnight. This helps draw out any impurities and also helps the flour to adhere to the livers better.

2 Drain the buttermilk from the livers, discarding the liquid. The livers need to be cooked last, so set aside until needed.

3 In a large sauté pan over medium heat, cook the bacon for about 5 minutes, until crisp. Remove the bacon with a slotted spoon to a plate, leaving the rendered fat in the pan. Raise the heat to medium-high, add the mushrooms, and cook for about 1 minute, or until golden brown. You don't want to crowd the pan when searing the mushrooms, so you might have to do this stage in batches. Remove the mushrooms with a slotted spoon to the plate with the bacon.

4 Add the wine to the pan and boil until reduced by three-quarters. Add the chicken broth and boil to reduce by half. Add the butter and return the mushrooms and bacon to the pan. Stir in the parsley. The sauce should be reduced to a glaze that just coats the mushrooms and bacon. Check and adjust for seasoning, adding salt and pepper if needed. Keep the sauce warm while preparing the livers.

5 Heat a large sauté pan over medium-high heat. Add enough canola oil so it coats the bottom of the pan. Season the drained chicken livers with salt and pepper, dredge with flour, and shake off any excess. When the oil is hot, add the livers to the pan, being careful not to crowd the pan; you may need to work in batches. And be careful! The livers pop and splatter while frying. Cook for about 1 minute per side, or until golden brown but still rosy in the centers.

6 Put the chicken livers on a large platter, spoon over the mushroom and bacon sauce, and serve with a bowl of soft polenta.

SPICY SRIRACHA CHICKEN WINGS

These are the wings we make and sell at B Spot, and they are super popular despite being super spicy. If you don't have a bottle of Sriracha on hand, get one. It is an amazing and amazingly versatile condiment that goes great in soups, on sandwiches, and on pretty much everything else! It is what gives these wings their signature kick.

5 pounds chicken wings, split

¼ cup coriander seeds, crushed

1 teaspoon cumin seeds, crushed

1 teaspoon ground cinnamon

2 tablespoons kosher salt

¼ cup extra-virgin olive oil

¾ cup Sriracha sauce

12 tablespoons (1½ sticks) unsalted butter, melted

½ cup chopped fresh cilantro

Grated zest and juice of 3 limes

Vegetable oil, for deep-frying

1 In a very large bowl, toss to combine the wings, coriander, cumin, cinnamon, salt, and olive oil. Cover and refrigerate for at least 4 hours or overnight.

2 Preheat the oven to 375°F.

3 Arrange the wings on 3 large rimmed baking sheets and roast for 30 minutes, or until firm but not fully cooked through. (If you would prefer not to deep-fry the wings as this recipe states, continue baking for an additional hour, or until the wings are crisp and golden brown.)

4 Meanwhile, in a mixing bowl, stir to combine the Sriracha, melted butter, cilantro, and lime zest and juice.

5 In a deep-fryer or very large pot, heat 8 inches vegetable oil to 375°F.

6 In batches, fry the wings for 5 minutes, or until crisp and golden brown. When done, remove the wings from the oil, shaking off as much oil as possible. As each batch is cooked, toss the wings in the Sriracha-butter sauce, remove, and transfer to a platter.

7 Serve hot, with plenty of napkins.

SMOKY & SPICY CHICKEN WINGS

Fried chicken wings are a delicious treat. When I have a little extra time, I like to smoke the wings before frying them. You end up with wings that start off smoky and then finish with a blast of heat. Sounds like the perfect football food if you ask me.

2 tablespoons extra-virgin olive oil

Juice of 3 limes

1 tablespoon smoked paprika

Pinch of sugar

Kosher salt

5 pounds chicken wings, split

¼ cup Sriracha sauce, or more to taste

1 tablespoon honey, or more to taste

Splash of cider vinegar

4 cups duck fat or canola oil

4 tablespoons (½ stick) unsalted butter

1 In a large zip-top bag, combine the olive oil, the juice of 2 of the limes, the paprika, sugar, and a big pinch of salt. Add the chicken wings and toss to combine. Marinate for at least 1 hour or overnight in the refrigerator.

2 Soak apple-wood chips in water for 30 minutes. Prepare and set a smoker to 275°F (see opposite).

3 Smoke the wings for 30 minutes.

4 Meanwhile, in a large saucepan over medium heat, combine the Sriracha, honey, and vinegar. When the sauce is heated through, season with salt.

5 In a deep cast-iron pot, such as a Dutch oven, over medium-high heat, heat the duck fat to 350°F, using a deep-fry thermometer to monitor the temperature. (Alternatively, you can bake the wings in a 450°F oven for 3 to 5 minutes.)

6 Fry the wings in batches, flipping once, for 4 minutes, or until crispy on all sides. As they finish cooking, move the wings to the pan of hot sauce. Add the butter and stir to coat. Stir in the juice of the remaining lime.

7 Taste the sauce and adjust the salt, honey, and hot sauce if desired. Serve hot.

SMOKING

I am obsessed with smoking food. When done correctly, it adds a unique and pleasant flavor to meats. And by combining various woods, rubs, brines, and glazes, you can customize the entire process to your liking. Many people oversmoke their foods, with the smoke flavor overpowering the meat, which should be the star of the show. I think it's helpful to think of smoke as a type of seasoning, providing another layer of subtle flavor. This is why I prefer to use fruitwoods like apple; they are sweeter and milder. Soak them in cold water for at least half an hour before draining and using.

Expensive smokers do make things easier, but you don't need them. I've made smokers out of regular grills, old stainless-steel beer coolers, and sheet pans on the stovetop. The easiest way to give great smoky flavor to foods cooked on a gas grill is by wrapping wood chips or chunks in heavy-duty foil and tossing them under the cooking grate. Make sure you poke some holes in the pouch to allow the smoke to escape, and keep the grill lid closed for the first 15 minutes or so. To create a stovetop smoker, put soaked wood chips in the bottom of a hotel pan (or chafing dish insert) and top with a shallow perforated pan. Put the meat in the perforated pan, cover the pan tightly with foil, and put over medium-high heat to create smoke.

The two main types of smoking are cold and hot. Cold smoking, typically done at temperatures lower than 120°F, is used when the goal is to flavor food without cooking it. Think of cured fish, such as salmon, or foods like sausage that will be fully cooked later on. Hot smoking is what we normally think of as barbecue, where foods are cooked in the presence of smoke at temperatures around 200°F. To transform tough briskets and pork butts into mouthwateringly tender meat, you need to cook the meat "low and slow."

CORIANDER-AND-ORANGE-ROASTED CHICKEN

There's almost nothing better than a perfectly roasted chicken. In my first cookbook, *Live to Cook*, I included my wife Lizzie's roasted chicken, a definite favorite. This recipe is slightly different in that the bird is marinated for a couple of hours instead of being preseasoned. It also yields great results, with a nice touch of heat. The beauty of roasted chicken is that you can make several dishes starting with one master recipe—Lizzie and I like to have this for dinner one night and then later in the week use the leftovers to make Pulled Chicken Salad with Almonds, Apples & Dried Cherries (page 162) for lunch or Chicken Pot Pie (page 164) for dinner.

1 (3-pound) chicken

Grated zest and juice of
1 orange

4 tablespoons olive oil

1 tablespoon honey

2 tablespoons coriander
seeds, toasted

1 garlic clove, minced, plus
3 whole cloves

1 jalapeño, minced

1 orange, thinly sliced and
seeded

2 bay leaves, preferably fresh

1 small red onion, peeled

1 small bunch fresh thyme

1 Rinse the chicken under cold water and pat dry. Whisk together the orange zest and juice, 2 tablespoons of the olive oil, the honey, coriander seeds, the minced garlic, and the jalapeño. Put the chicken in a large nonreactive bowl or gallon-sized zip-top bag, pour the marinade over the chicken, and rub it all over the inside and outside of the bird. Refrigerate for at least 3 hours or overnight, occasionally turning the chicken in the marinade.

2 Remove the chicken from the fridge half an hour before roasting so that it comes to room temperature. Preheat the oven to 425°F.

3 Put the chicken in a large roasting pan breast-side-up. Loosen the skin of the chicken breast and wedge 1 or 2 orange slices and a bay leaf under the skin of each breast half. Put the onion, the whole garlic cloves, the thyme, and the remaining orange slices in the cavity of the chicken and, in the case of the orange slices and thyme, around the chicken in the roasting pan as well. Rub the entire chicken liberally with the remaining 2 tablespoons olive oil.

4 Roast for 45 minutes to 1 hour, until the chicken reaches an internal temperature of 160°F (check one of the thighs) and the juices run clear.

5 Remove from the oven and let rest for 10 to 20 minutes. Discard the aromatics from the pan and cavity. Cut the chicken into 8 pieces and serve immediately.

TWICE-FRIED OLD BAY CHICKEN WITH SRIRACHA-HONEY

Many of my favorite recipes are based on food memories from my childhood. This one is no exception. I can still vividly recall a family vacation to Baltimore when I was around twelve years old. What I remember most, in addition to talking sports and playing catch with my cousins, was the amazing boiled crab and fried chicken. Everything was pretty heavily seasoned with Old Bay, which back then was a totally new flavor to me. Even today, the flavor of Old Bay instantly takes me back to that trip. This is my take on a delicious childhood memory.

2 tablespoons Old Bay seasoning

1 teaspoon smoked paprika

1 teaspoon chipotle powder

1 tablespoon cracked coriander seeds

2 (3-pound) chickens, cut into 12 parts each (4 split breast pieces, 2 legs, 2 thighs, 2 wings, 2 split backbone pieces)

2 quarts rendered lard or peanut oil

½ cup Sriracha sauce

½ cup honey

1½ cups all-purpose flour

2 tablespoons cornstarch

1 tablespoon kosher salt

1 The night before cooking, combine the Old Bay, paprika, chipotle powder, and coriander seeds in a gallon-sized zip-top bag. Add the chicken pieces and shake to coat with the spices. Refrigerate overnight.

2 Allow the chicken to come to room temperature for half an hour before cooking.

3 In a large Dutch oven, heat the lard to 340°F.

4 Stir together the Sriracha and honey and set aside.

5 Combine the flour, cornstarch, and salt. Dredge the chicken with the flour mixture. Begin adding the chicken to the hot lard, starting with the thighs. Continue adding the chicken pieces until the pot is full, but not crowded. When the pot is full, put the lid on. The chicken will need to be cooked in batches.

6 After 3 minutes, uncover the pot and flip the pieces. Put the lid back on and cook for an additional 3 minutes. When done, remove the chicken to a cooling rack and repeat the process with the remaining chicken.

7 Once all the chicken is done, raise the temperature of the lard to 365°F. Fry the chicken, uncovered, in batches for 2 minutes per side, or until golden and crispy. When done, drain on paper towels and serve immediately with the Sriracha-honey.

GRILLED CHICKEN THIGHS WITH PEACHES, MINT & ALMONDS

When it comes to chicken, I have to admit that I'm a thigh guy. Chicken thighs have the deepest flavor of all the cuts on the bird, and they always seem to come out tender and juicy. As a bonus, they also happen to be the cheapest part of the bird. This is a great summer dish that capitalizes on ripe ingredients at the top of their game. It's big on flavor, but low on hassle—my kind of recipe. If you plan ahead, you can get this on the table for friends and family on a weeknight.

1 tablespoon coriander seeds, toasted and ground

1 tablespoon smoked paprika

Kosher salt

10 bone-in, skin-on chicken thighs

¼ cup extra-virgin olive oil, plus more for brushing

½ cup thinly sliced red onion

6 peaches, pitted and each cut into 8 pieces

1 jalapeño, seeds and ribs removed, minced

Grated zest and juice of 2 limes

2 cups arugula

1 cup thinly sliced fresh mint

½ cup Marcona almonds, chopped

1 Combine the coriander, paprika, and 1 tablespoon salt in a large zip-top bag. Add the chicken thighs, turn to coat on all sides, and refrigerate overnight.

2 Allow the chicken to come to room temperature for 30 minutes before cooking. Pat the chicken dry.

3 Heat a charcoal or gas grill so that one side is medium-high and the other very low.

4 Brush the chicken thighs with a little olive oil and put skin-side-down on the hot side of the grill. Cover the grill. After 2 minutes, remove the lid, flip the chicken, and put it on the cooler side of the grill. Put the lid back on and cook for 15 to 20 minutes, until the chicken hits an internal temperature of 160°F.

5 Meanwhile, in a medium bowl, combine the onion, peaches, and jalapeño. In a separate bowl, whisk together the lime zest and juice, the ¼ cup olive oil, and a good pinch of salt. Pour the dressing over the peaches and gently toss to combine. Add the arugula, mint, and almonds and toss once or twice.

6 To serve, put the chicken thighs on a large platter. Top with the peach mixture and serve immediately.

BRAISED CHICKEN THIGHS WITH SPICY KALE

Serves
6

In the restaurant biz, it isn't too often that you get a couple of nights off to spend with visiting friends. But last winter, we got to do just that when our dear friends Laurence Kretchmer and his wife, Becca Parish, came to stay with us in Cleveland, bringing along their lovely young daughter, Delilah. After a few days of hitting the town, we decided to stay in for dinner. While Kretchmer is a front-of-the-house guy, he wanted to prove to me he had chops in the kitchen. I'm not sure how famous his "famous" chicken and kale is outside his own family, but I can tell you it's delicious. (And I may have made it once or twice after he left town.)

Kosher salt

6 bone-in, skin-on chicken thighs

2 tablespoons olive oil

2 cups thinly sliced red onions

2 cups large-diced peeled carrots

1 jalapeño, sliced into rings

4 garlic cloves, sliced

1½ cups dry white wine

1 (12-ounce) can crushed San Marzano tomatoes

2 bay leaves, fresh or dried

2 pounds kale, roughly chopped

½ cup toasted fresh bread crumbs

Grated zest of 2 lemons

½ cup chopped fresh flat-leaf parsley

2 tablespoons extra-virgin olive oil

1 If you have the time, liberally salt the chicken the night before and refrigerate overnight.

2 Allow the chicken to come to room temperature for half an hour before cooking. Pat the chicken dry.

3 Preheat the oven to 375°F.

4 In a large Dutch oven, heat the olive oil over medium heat. When the oil is hot, put the chicken skin-side-down into the pot. Cook for 3 to 4 minutes, until the chicken is well browned. Flip the pieces and cook for 3 to 4 minutes to brown the other sides. Remove the chicken from the pot and set aside on a plate.

5 Add the onions and a good pinch of salt to the pot and cook for 1 minute. Add the carrots, jalapeño, and garlic and cook for 2 minutes. Pour in the wine and scrape up the tasty browned bits from the bottom of the pan using a wooden spoon. Cook for about 4 minutes, or until the wine is reduced by half. Add the tomatoes and bay leaves and bring to a simmer.

6 Adjust for seasoning, adding salt if needed, and then add the kale. Cover the pot and cook for 5 minutes. Remove the lid and stir. Put the chicken thighs on top of the kale, put the lid back on, and put in the oven for 20 minutes, until the chicken is cooked through.

7 Meanwhile, in a small bowl, combine the bread crumbs, lemon zest, parsley, and extra-virgin olive oil.

8 Remove the chicken from the oven and discard the bay leaves. Top the chicken with the bread crumb mixture. Serve family-style right from the pot.

RIGATONI WITH CHICKEN LIVER SAUCE

A couple of years back, I was in Philly doing an Alex's Lemonade Stand fund-raiser. It is one of the best cooking events of the year for one of the best causes: funding the fight against childhood cancer. The night before the big event, host chef Marc Vetri and his chef-partner, Jeff Michaud, hosted a family-style dinner for all participating chefs, who traveled from all over to take part. Well-known chefs and restaurateurs sat together at big tables, feasting on great food. In my opinion, nobody puts out better pasta dishes than Vetri, and for his second course, he knocked it outta the park. As everybody was going crazy over the rigatoni with chicken liver sauce, I glanced over at Bobby Flay, who looked at me and said, "It's so good, I'm actually getting mad." It's dishes and moments like these that make cooking and the restaurant biz so special to me. Here is my best shot at Vetri's killer pasta.

Kosher salt

1 pound dried rigatoni

1 pound pancetta, diced

2 shallots, minced

2 pounds chicken livers, cleaned and chopped

1 cup chopped fresh flat-leaf parsley

1 tablespoon unsalted butter

¼ cup freshly grated Parmesan cheese

2 tablespoons extra-virgin olive oil

1 Bring a large pot of salted water to boil for the pasta. Add the rigatoni and cook for about 8 minutes, until al dente. Drain, reserving 1 cup of the pasta water.

2 Meanwhile, put a large sauté pan over medium heat. Add the pancetta and cook until it is almost crisp, about 10 minutes. Add the shallots and cook for 1 minute. With a slotted spoon, remove the pancetta mixture from the pan and set aside on a plate.

3 Raise the heat under the pan to high. Season the chicken livers with a pinch of salt and add them to the pan. Sauté the livers for about 1 minute. Add the reserved 1 cup pasta water to the pan and reduce the heat to low. With a wooden spoon, scrape up the tasty bits on the bottom of the pan. Return the pancetta mixture to the pan and raise the heat to medium. Add the rigatoni and toss well to combine.

4 Remove from the heat and add the parsley, butter, Parmesan, and olive oil. Stir and serve immediately.

GRILLED MARINATED CHICKEN BREASTS

I know, I know. . . . All anybody wants to eat lately are chicken breasts. It's no secret that I'm not the biggest fan of this ultra-lean, ultra-mild cut of meat. But the least you can do to appease me is promise to cook chicken breasts bone-in and skin-on—that's where all of the flavor is! If you really *must* eat a boneless, skinless chicken breast, you can always remove the skin and bones after cooking. You gotta at least give the poor little guy a fighting chance at some flavor! The Greek-inspired marinade helps here, too; serve with Feta & Cucumber Salad (page 219).

6 bone-in, skin-on chicken breast halves

Kosher salt

1 cup Greek yogurt

3 garlic cloves, minced

Grated zest and juice of 1 orange

1 tablespoon coriander seeds, toasted and ground

2 teaspoons cumin seeds, toasted and ground

2 teaspoons smoked paprika

2 teaspoons chipotle powder

1 cup chopped fresh cilantro

1 Rinse the chicken under cold water and pat dry. Season the breasts liberally with salt. In a gallon-sized zip-top bag, combine the yogurt, garlic, orange zest and juice, coriander, cumin, paprika, chipotle, and cilantro. Add the chicken, turn to coat, and refrigerate for 2 to 4 hours.

2 Let the chicken come to room temperature for 30 minutes before grilling.

3 Meanwhile, heat a charcoal or gas grill to medium.

4 Remove the chicken from the bag, wiping off and discarding any excess marinade. Put the chicken on the grill skin-side-down and cover with the lid. Grill for 7 to 8 minutes, open the lid, and flip the bird. Put the lid back on and grill for 10 to 12 minutes, until the chicken reaches an internal temp of 160°F.

5 Let rest for 10 minutes before serving.

BBQ CHICKEN LEGS

As most of you probably know by now, I am a much bigger fan of dark meat than I am of white. Not only does the meat have more flavor and come out juicier, but it stands up better to boldly flavored sauces. In this recipe, I pair chicken drumsticks with a chipotle-laced barbecue sauce. Since the sauce is a little on the sweet side, I like to balance it out with a citrusy Grilled-Corn Salad (page 217).

½ cup extra-virgin olive oil

¼ cup fresh lime juice

2 garlic cloves, minced

1 jalapeño, seeds and ribs removed, minced

Kosher salt

Freshly ground black pepper

12 chicken legs

¾ cup Cleveland BBQ Sauce (page 100)

Fresh cilantro sprigs and lime wedges, for serving

1 In a gallon-sized zip-top bag, combine the olive oil, lime juice, garlic, jalapeño, and salt. Add the chicken legs, turn to coat, and refrigerate overnight.

2 Heat a charcoal or gas grill to medium-high.

3 Season the chicken legs with salt and pepper; put them on the grill and cover the grill with the lid. After 8 minutes, flip the chicken legs and put the lid back down. Continue cooking the chicken for 8 to 10 minutes, basting the legs with the barbecue sauce during the last 3 minutes. Remove to a platter to rest.

4 Garnish the chicken legs with cilantro sprigs and lime wedges before serving.

BRICK-GRILLED CHICKEN

During the summer, I spend as much time cooking outside as possible. That means firing up the grill, keeping things simple, and feeding whoever stops by. This recipe is one of our favorite grilled-chicken dishes. It is a twist on my mom's Greek-style chicken, except we shift it to the grill and add a couple of bricks to make sure it comes out flat and crisp. (If the weather isn't cooperating, this recipe also works well on a grill pan.) Like any great summertime recipe, it's quick, easy, delicious, and—served with Fregola in Tomato Sauce (page 245)—feeds a small crowd.

2 (3-pound) chickens

1 cup olive oil

¼ cup fresh lemon juice

6 garlic cloves, minced

2 tablespoons chopped fresh oregano

Kosher salt

1 To butterfly each chicken, put it breast-side-down on a work surface. Using a sharp knife or pair of kitchen shears, cut along both sides of the backbone and neck to fully remove them. (Reserve these for later use in stock or soup.) Flip over the chicken and firmly press down on the breastbone to flatten it.

2 In a large bowl, whisk together the oil, lemon juice, garlic, and oregano. Add the chickens to this mixture, turning to coat. Cover and refrigerate for at least 3 hours or overnight.

3 Heat a charcoal or gas grill to medium. (If you do not have access to a grill, use a heavy grill pan instead. Allow it to get very hot before adding the chickens.) Wrap 2 bricks in a double layer of aluminum foil.

4 Remove the chickens from the marinade, pat them dry, and season with salt on both sides. Put the chickens skin-side-down on the grill. Put a brick on top of each one to weight it down. Grill for 10 minutes. Remove the bricks, flip the chickens, and replace the bricks. Cover the grill and cook for 10 minutes, until the thighs register 160°F.

5 Remove the chickens from the grill and let rest for 10 minutes. Cut the chickens into quarters and serve on a platter.

PULLED CHICKEN SALAD WITH ALMONDS, APPLES & DRIED CHERRIES

I love this chicken salad: It's bright, refreshing, and slightly tart from the yogurt and Granny Smith apples. The dried cherries add a touch of sweetness, while the almonds provide a nice crunchy texture. Try this salad on a good-quality baguette with some peppery watercress or arugula for an excellent sandwich.

Coriander-and-Orange-Roasted-Chicken (page 148)

1 cup Greek yogurt

1 Granny Smith apple, cored and cut into small dice

½ cup dried tart cherries, roughly chopped

½ cup slivered almonds, toasted

¼ cup chopped fresh mint

Kosher salt

Remove the meat from the roasted chicken, discarding the bones and skin (or eating the skin as a snack). Chop the meat into medium pieces, or shred with your hands, and put into a large bowl. Add the yogurt, apple, cherries, almonds, and mint and season with salt. Toss with your hands to combine.

CHICKEN BROTH

I always have a stash of homemade chicken broth in the fridge or freezer. It's so easy to make and, in my mind, irreplaceable in soups, sauces, and hearty braises. I whip up a big batch once a month on a Sunday and freeze it in smaller containers. That way, there's always some on hand whenever a recipe calls for chicken broth. If you have any parsley stems sitting around, go ahead and toss those in, too.

2 pounds chicken backs and necks

2 pounds chicken feet (or additional backs and necks)

2 large red onions, quartered

2 large carrots, peeled and thickly sliced

1 head garlic, halved crosswise

4 sprigs fresh thyme

2 bay leaves, fresh or dried

1 tablespoon coriander seeds

1 tablespoon kosher salt

1 tablespoon black peppercorns

1 Rinse the chicken parts thoroughly in cold water. In a 10-quart stockpot, combine the chicken parts with 1½ gallons cold water and heat over high heat. Bring to a boil, skimming off any foam that rises to the top. Reduce the heat so that the water simmers, and cook for 2 hours, occasionally skimming off any foam.

2 Add the onions, carrots, garlic, thyme, bay leaves, coriander, salt, and peppercorns. Simmer for 2 hours, skimming off any fat that collects on the surface.

3 Strain the broth through a fine-mesh sieve into a large pot, discarding the solids. Quickly chill the broth by placing the pot in a sink full of ice water. When cool, divide into freezer-safe containers and store in the freezer until needed, or for up to a month or two.

CHICKEN POT PIE

Serves
12

Chicken pot pie may be the ultimate comfort food. This dish is perfect for a lazy Sunday watching football, because you can bake it before people come over and it stays hot forever. I know making dough from scratch sounds like a huge pain; it is worth it, but if the homemade dough is the only thing preventing you from trying this recipe, I give you a pass to use store-bought puff pastry. I won't tell if you won't.

1 cup pearl onions

3 recipes Coriander-and-Orange-Roasted Chicken (page 148)

12 tablespoons (1½ sticks) unsalted butter

2 cups finely diced yellow onions

10 garlic cloves, minced

¾ cup all-purpose flour, plus more for rolling

5 cups chicken broth, preferably homemade (page 163), warmed

2 cups finely diced carrots

Kosher salt and freshly ground black pepper

2 cups peas, preferably fresh

½ cup finely chopped fresh flat-leaf parsley

¼ cup finely chopped fresh tarragon

¼ cup heavy cream

½ recipe Pastry Dough (page 68)

1 large egg, beaten with 1 tablespoon milk

Flaky sea salt, such as Cyprus Flake or Maldon, and cracked black peppercorns

1 Bring a small saucepan of water to a boil. Add the pearl onions and boil for 2 minutes. Drain and, when cool enough to handle, peel the onions.

2 Remove the meat from the roasted chicken, discarding the bones and skin (or eating the skin as a snack). Chop the meat into medium pieces and put into a large bowl. You should end up with about 8 cups of cubed chicken. Set aside until needed.

3 Preheat the oven to 375°F.

4 In a large Dutch oven over medium-low heat, melt the butter. Add the diced onions and the garlic, and sauté for 15 minutes, or until translucent. Reduce the heat to low, add the flour, and cook, stirring constantly, for 2 minutes. Whisk in the hot chicken broth. Simmer over low heat for about 3 minutes, or until the broth begins to thicken and bubble slightly.

5 Add the carrots, 2 teaspoons kosher salt, and ½ teaspoon ground pepper and cook for 2 minutes. Add the pearl onions, peas, chicken, parsley, tarragon, and cream and simmer for 5 minutes. Taste and adjust for seasoning, adding salt and pepper if needed.

6 Divide the chicken mixture among 12 individual 2-cup molds and set aside while you roll out the dough.

7 On a floured surface, roll out each piece of dough until ⅛ inch thick. Cut into 12 (8-inch) circles. Lay a piece of dough over the top of each pot pie, letting it drape over the sides. Brush the tops and outside edges of each crust with the egg wash. Make 3 slits in the top of each piece of dough for steam vents. Sprinkle with sea salt and cracked peppercorns.

8 Put the pies on a baking sheet and bake for about 15 to 20 minutes, or until the tops are golden brown and the filling is bubbling hot.

AVGOLEMONO

I swear this soup is magical. At the first sign of a cold when I was growing up, my mom would put on a big pot of avgolemono. Soon, the whole house would fill with an intoxicating aroma, and two bowls later, I'd feel better than ever. (This soup is so good, in fact, that I might have faked illness on more than one occasion just to get a steaming bowl full.) To this day, whenever somebody in my family is feeling a little under the weather, I get out my biggest pot and start this recipe. What makes this version so good is the double broth—a whole chicken cooked in chicken broth. My mom would also cheat a bit by adding some flour to the whisked eggs, which helps prevent them from scrambling. The addition of fresh dill at the end is all mine . . . not that I'd dare add it when making it for my mom. What an earful I'd get!

1 (3-pound) chicken

1 bay leaf, fresh or dried

3 quarts chicken broth, preferably homemade (page 163)

1 cup orzo pasta

Kosher salt

Grated zest and juice of 3 lemons

2 tablespoons Wondra flour

2 large eggs

½ cup chopped fresh dill

1 Put the chicken, bay leaf, and broth in a large stockpot and bring to a simmer. Cook for about 1½ hours, until the chicken is fully cooked. Remove the chicken to a platter to cool.

2 Add the orzo to the simmering broth and cook for 10 minutes. Check the broth for seasoning and add salt as needed.

3 Meanwhile, cut up the chicken, discarding the bones and skin.

4 In a medium bowl, whisk together the lemon zest and juice and the flour. Whisk in the eggs. Add a little of the simmering broth and whisk again. Check that the heat underneath the pot is low and then whisk in the egg mixture. The soup will become cloudy and thicken slightly. Once the eggs have been added, it's important not to allow the soup to boil, as this will scramble the eggs, making the soup look more like egg drop.

5 Add the chicken to the soup along with the dill. Discard the bay leaf. Serve immediately.

CHICKEN LIVER BREAD DUMPLINGS IN BROTH

This is such a tasty soup that's not only quick and easy to make, but also uses many ingredients that home cooks tend to waste. Old bread, extra broth, and reserved chicken livers should never be thrown away—especially when they can be combined into this fulfilling soup in practically no time flat! And any leftover dumplings are great for breakfast split in half and fried with eggs in butter.

4 quarts chicken broth, preferably homemade (page 163)

4 cups day-old bread, crusts removed, cut into small dice

½ cup whole milk, at room temperature

1½ teaspoons unsalted butter

½ cup minced yellow onion

1 small garlic clove, minced

Kosher salt

2 ounces chicken livers, finely chopped

1 large egg, lightly beaten

¼ cup chopped fresh flat-leaf parsley

Grated zest of ½ lemon

Pinch of grated nutmeg

½ cup plain dried bread crumbs (if needed)

1 Pour the broth into a large pot and bring to a simmer.

2 Meanwhile, in a large mixing bowl, combine the bread and milk.

3 In a sauté pan over medium heat, cook the butter, onion, garlic, and a pinch of salt for about 2 minutes, or until the onion and garlic are softened. Remove from the heat and set aside to cool.

4 Add the onion mixture to the bread along with the livers, egg, parsley, lemon zest, nutmeg, and a pinch of salt. Mix thoroughly with your hands until the dumplings come together. They should be quite sticky, but not wet. Form a test dumpling about the size of a golf ball and drop it into the simmering broth. After a few minutes, take a look at the dumpling: If it is holding together, you are set. If it is breaking apart, mix in ¼ cup of the bread crumbs and form and cook another test dumpling. Repeat if necessary until a test dumpling holds together. It is unlikely you'll need to use all of the remaining bread crumbs.

5 Form the rest of the dumplings any size you prefer. Making them in 1-tablespoon portions will yield about 22 golf-ball-sized dumplings. Having wet hands makes this process easier. When all the dumplings are formed, put them in the simmering broth and cook for 30 minutes.

6 Put a few cooked dumplings in each bowl and top with the simmering broth. Serve immediately.

CHICKEN & FETA SAUSAGE

Makes
4
pounds

The key to making delicious chicken sausages is to use flavorful chicken thighs and a good amount of pork fat. I love this recipe in particular because it combines my favorite Greek tastes: bright mint, acidic lemon, and salty feta. In summertime, grill these sausages until crisp on the outside and serve alongside a refreshing tomato salad (see page 207). This sausage is so tasty, it almost gives pork sausage a run for the money.

2 tablespoons kosher salt

1 tablespoon coriander seeds, toasted and ground

2 garlic cloves, minced

¼ cup chopped fresh mint

Grated zest of 3 lemons

3 pounds skinless chicken thigh meat, cut into large dice

1 pound fatback, cut into large dice

¼ cup dry white wine, cold

¼ cup extra-virgin olive oil

½ cup crumbled feta cheese

6 feet of hog casing, soaked overnight and rinsed (see page 35), optional

1 Combine the salt, coriander, garlic, mint, and lemon zest. Season the cubed chicken and fatback with the spice mixture, put in a gallon-sized zip-top bag, and refrigerate overnight.

2 Thoroughly chill all the sausage-grinding equipment, the mixing bowl, and the paddle attachment. Grind the chilled meat mixture through the small die into the mixing bowl. Using the paddle attachment, mix in the wine, olive oil, and feta. Refrigerate until ready to use or for up to 2 days.

3 Stuff this sausage filling into a hog casing (see page 36) and poach in simmering water or grill until the sausage reaches an internal temperature of 160°F; form into patties and pan-roast until browned and cooked through; or leave it loose to crumble into other recipes.

TURKEY & SAGE SAUSAGE

If you are planning on making Smoked Turkey Breast (page 171), buy a whole turkey and reserve the legs and thighs for sausage. For starters, it is much cheaper to butcher your own bird. More importantly, turkey sausage tastes so much better than turkey breast! As in the case of Chicken & Feta Sausage (opposite), this recipe benefits from the addition of pork fat. I've attempted it without it and the sausage ends up dry and lifeless. Let's face it, Julia Child was onto something!

3 pounds skinless turkey leg and thigh meat, cut into large dice

1 pound fatback, cut into large dice

3 tablespoons kosher salt

½ cup chopped fresh sage

¼ cup chopped fresh chives

2 garlic cloves, minced

Grated zest of 1 orange

1 tablespoon ground black pepper

Small pinch of grated nutmeg

½ cup whole milk, cold

½ cup dry white wine, cold

6 feet of hog casing, soaked overnight and rinsed (see page 35), optional

1 Combine the turkey, fatback, salt, sage, chives, garlic, orange zest, pepper, and nutmeg in a gallon-sized zip-top bag and refrigerate overnight.

2 Thoroughly chill all the sausage-grinding equipment, the mixing bowl, and the paddle attachment. Grind the chilled meat mixture through the small die into the mixing bowl. Using the paddle attachment, mix in the milk and wine. Refrigerate until ready to use or for up to 2 days.

3 Stuff this sausage filling into a hog casing (see page 36) and poach in simmering water or grill until the sausage reaches an internal temperature of 160°F; form into patties and pan-roast until browned and cooked through; or leave it loose and use as a substitute for the lamb in Lamb Bolognese with Cavatelli (page 134).

SMOKED TURKEY BREAST

Believe it or not, it is acceptable to eat and enjoy turkey at times other than Thanksgiving. I really love turkey—as long as somebody isn't trying to pass it off as "bacon" or a healthy version of hamburger. One of my favorite ways to enjoy turkey breast is smoked and sliced in a sandwich with good bread, ripe tomato, mayo, basil, and *real* bacon. This recipe is pretty easy to master, and by smoking the meat on the bone, you end up with the tastiest meat possible. If you don't have the time or equipment to smoke the meat, go ahead and roast it in a 350°F oven until it hits 160°F inside, about 1 hour.

1 bone-in, skin-on turkey breast half (about 5 pounds)

3 garlic cloves, peeled

1 tablespoon kosher salt

½ cup chopped fresh tarragon

½ cup chopped fresh flat-leaf parsley

Grated zest of 2 lemons

2 tablespoons extra-virgin olive oil

1 Rinse the turkey breast under cold water and pat dry. In a mortar and pestle, smash the garlic with the salt, tarragon, parsley, and lemon zest to form a paste. Mix in the olive oil. Thoroughly rub this mixture all over the turkey breast. Put the turkey in a gallon-sized zip-top bag and refrigerate overnight or for up to 48 hours.

2 Prepare and set a smoker to 200°F, using apple-wood chips.

3 Smoke the turkey breast until it reaches an internal temperature of 160°F. This should take 2½ to 3 hours. When done, remove the turkey from the smoker and let rest for at least 30 minutes.

4 To serve, slice the breast thinly and build your favorite sandwiches. The turkey will keep, covered, for about 4 days in the fridge.

DEEP-FRIED TURKEY

When it comes to Thanksgiving turkey, I have to admit that I'm usually a traditionalist. But that doesn't mean I don't like to mix it up occasionally. And when I do, there's nothing better than a crispy deep-fried bird. While deep-frying a whole turkey requires more than a little caution, the results include ridiculously crunchy skin and moist, flavorful meat. Better yet, the bird's done in a fraction of the time of roasting!

1 (10-pound) turkey

¼ cup chopped fresh sage

¼ cup kosher salt

1 tablespoon coriander seeds, toasted and ground

1 tablespoon garlic powder

1 tablespoon smoked paprika

1 tablespoon chipotle powder

2 teaspoons celery seeds

1 teaspoon cumin seeds, toasted and ground

3 to 5 gallons peanut oil, depending upon your fryer

1 Rinse the turkey inside and out with cold water and pat it dry. Mix to combine the sage, salt, coriander, garlic powder, paprika, chipotle powder, celery seeds, and cumin. Rub this mixture all over the turkey, inside and out. Cover the turkey and refrigerate overnight to let the seasonings penetrate the meat.

2 The following day, remove the turkey from the refrigerator about 45 minutes before cooking. Thoroughly pat the turkey dry, making sure to get into the cavity with a towel to soak up as much moisture as possible. (Water splatters in the deep fryer!)

3 Set up the turkey-fryer outside, on a heatproof surface that you don't mind splattering and away from any structures. Pour in peanut oil up to the maximum fill line. Heat the oil to 350°F.

4 Very slowly and carefully lower the turkey into the oil, making sure it is completely submerged. Fry the turkey for 30 to 35 minutes. Carefully remove to a roasting-rack-lined baking sheet to allow the bird to drain and rest for about 10 minutes.

5 Carve and serve with your favorite Thanksgiving sides and salads.

FRYING

They say you can deep-fry an old shoe and it will taste good. While I doubt that's true, I do believe that almost everything else tastes better when properly fried in fat. Granted, it's not the healthiest way to cook, but can we agree that it is one of the most delicious? If you fry in moderation (so, no, not every day, I am sorry to say), I think you can indulge a bit.

I do almost all of my frying in naturally rendered animal fats—pork lard being my favorite, but also beef tallow and duck fat. First of all, they produce a tastier final result; nothing tops a potato fried in lard! But they also have a higher smoke point than many other fats, which means you can fry foods at the ideal temperature of 365° to 370°F without fear of the oil burning. This gives you crispy, grease-free food.

There are two main types of frying: deep and shallow. When deep-frying, you want enough fat to fully cover the food, approximately four times the amount of what's going in. The large amount not only allows for even cooking all around the food, but also maintains a more consistent temperature when the food is added. Once added to the oil, the food should not be on top of another piece. Pay close attention until the food becomes deep golden brown. If cooked properly, fried items shouldn't even need to be drained on paper towels. But do immediately season the food as soon as it comes out of the fryer.

With shallow-frying, the fat should come about halfway up the sides of the food being fried. Done right, shallow-frying leaves foods like chicken wings just as crunchy as deep-frying, but using a fraction of the fat. This method is also much quicker than deep frying because you don't have to wait for a whole pot of oil to heat up. (Not to mention the matter of storing the used oil.) But because there is less oil, it's best to fry the food in batches so you don't crowd the pan. When one side is golden brown, flip the ingredient. As with deep-frying, it's important to season the food as soon as it's pulled from the pan.

WHOLE SQUAB

DUCK FAT

VENISON CUBES

WHOLE QUAIL

GAME

RABBIT LEGS
(BONE-IN)

DUCK LIVERS

"**G**ame" is the word traditionally used for wild birds and animals like duck, boar, deer, and elk. These days, it more often refers to farm- or ranch-raised versions. There will always be a difference between the way truly wild animals and their farmed kin taste, as wild animals eat a broader range of foods and have greater depth of flavor.

If you happen to hunt your own game birds, you know how enjoyable and unique a truly wild squab, quail, or duck can taste. But because it isn't legal for hunters to sell wild game to restaurants, markets, or shoppers, most of us have to get our game birds by purchasing them from farms that raise them. That's just fine because not only is farm-raised game readily available, it's usually humanely raised (unlike a lot of chicken and turkey).

Duck is certainly the most popular game bird, but quail, pheasant, partridge, and goose all have unique and wonderful characteristics and I encourage you to seek them out. When buying duck for roasting, grilling, or braising, I prefer Long Island (also called Pekin), as I find it to be tender with a nice fat-to-meat ratio. I tend to reserve Muscovy duck for when I'm curing or smoking, as the thicker layer of fat and denser texture of the meat hold up better to these cooking methods. For notes on cooking various game bird cuts, see Cook It Right: Chicken, Turkey & Game Birds (page 142).

Farmed venison meat is milder in flavor than wild yet still red, lean, uniquely gamey, and pleasantly different from beef; elk is very similar in taste and texture. Though their meat looks like beef, it contains a lot less intramuscular fat, which dictates the way the meat needs to be cooked. Sausage, such as Venison & Dried Cherry Sausage (page 179), is a great way to prepare lean game meat because you can add fat to the recipe. Moist and slow stews, like Venison Stew (page 194) and Venison Sloppy Joes (page 193), are also tasty ways to use venison, elk, and other large game.

Some people describe the flavor of wild boar as "what pork used to taste like." A distant relative of the domesticated pig, boar boasts a much stronger but still familiar porkiness. Not surprisingly, boar works as a great substitute for pork in most recipes. For suggested cooking techniques, see Cook It Right: Pork (page 63).

Rabbits, like chicken, change in flavor and tenderness as they age. I cook small rabbits much as I do a young fryer chicken, as the meat of both is lean, tender, and mild. I approach older, larger rabbits like I do old hens, tossing them in the stew or braising pot. To keep lean rabbit from drying out, I like to braise it in red wine, such as in Braised Rabbit Thighs (page 200), or, better yet, bundle it in bacon and pan-roast it, as in the recipe for Bacon-Wrapped Rabbit Legs (page 197).

DUCK PASTRAMI

Serves 6

The first time I saw duck breast prepared in the style of pastrami was back in the late 1980s. It was done by chef David Burke, one of the most creative—and copied—chefs in the country at the time. Here is my remake of his classic dish. What is it they say about imitation being the sincerest form of flattery? If you can find it, use Muscovy duck breast for this recipe, as it's much bigger than the Long Island variety. Note that you'll need to start this recipe at least 3 days before you want to serve it. Serve the pastrami with Mustard Fruit (page 226) and grilled bread.

¼ cup kosher salt

2 tablespoons packed dark brown sugar

3 juniper berries

½ teaspoon mustard seeds

1 teaspoon black peppercorns

2 allspice berries

2 cloves

1 bay leaf, fresh or dried

1 Muscovy duck breast half or 2 Long Island duck breast halves (about 1 pound total)

1 In a saucepan, combine 4 cups water, the salt, brown sugar, juniper berries, mustard seeds, black peppercorns, allspice, cloves, and bay leaf and bring to a simmer. Cook for 5 minutes, whisking to fully dissolve the salt and sugar. Remove the brining liquid from the heat and let cool completely.

2 Put the duck into a gallon-sized zip-top bag, pour in the brine, and refrigerate for 48 hours.

3 Prepare and set a smoker to 200°F. I like apple-wood chips for this recipe.

4 Remove the duck from the brine, discarding the liquid. Rinse the breasts under cold water and pat dry. Put the duck skin-side-down in the smoker and cook until it reaches an internal temperature of 130°F, 20 to 30 minutes. Remove the duck from the smoker and let cool. Wrap in plastic wrap, and refrigerate overnight or for up to 1 week.

5 To serve, remove the duck from the fridge and slice it very thinly.

VENISON & DRIED CHERRY SAUSAGE

Makes
4
pounds

Although I am not a hunter, I do have lots of friends and family who enjoy the activity very much. That works out great for all of us—they hunt and I eat! Generally, they want to keep all the venison chops and loins, which leaves me all the shoulder and leg meat. It just so happens that the shoulder is the best cut to use for sausage, because of its densely flavored meat.

3 pounds trimmed venison shoulder, cut into large dice

1 pound fatback, cut into large dice

3 tablespoons kosher salt

½ cup chopped fresh flat-leaf parsley

2 garlic cloves, minced

Grated zest of 2 oranges

¼ teaspoon ground juniper berry

1 tablespoon freshly ground black pepper

Small pinch of grated nutmeg

½ cup whole milk, cold

½ cup dry white wine, cold

1 cup dried cherries, roughly chopped

6 feet of hog casing, soaked overnight and rinsed (see page 35), optional

1 Combine the venison, fatback, salt, parsley, garlic, orange zest, ground juniper berry, pepper, and nutmeg in a gallon-sized zip-top bag, turn to coat, and refrigerate overnight.

2 Thoroughly chill all the sausage-grinding equipment, the mixing bowl, and the paddle attachment. Grind the chilled meat mixture through the small die into the chilled mixing bowl. Using the paddle attachment, mix in the milk, wine, and cherries. Refrigerate until ready to use or for up to 1 week.

3 Stuff this sausage filling into a hog casing (see page 36) and poach in simmering water or grill until the sausage reaches an internal temperature of 160°F; form into patties and pan-roast until browned and cooked through; or leave it loose to crumble into other recipes.

DUCK LIVER MOUSSE MASON JARS WITH PICKLED CHERRIES

Makes 5 (4-ounce) jars

I love serving mousses and rillettes in Mason jars at parties. They can be made well ahead of time and pulled out just before your guests arrive, making you look like a rock star. This mousse, while still relatively simple, requires a bit more finesse than others, because it includes egg and is cooked in a water bath similar to a crème brûlée. But the amazing flavor of pickled tart cherries against the creamy silky mousse makes it totally worth the effort. Instead of Mason jars, you can bake these in ramekins and *brulée* the tops with sugar. That will definitely get your guests talking!

½ cup fresh orange juice

¼ cup Sauternes

1 shallot, minced

1 small garlic clove, minced

5 ounces duck liver, rinsed and cleaned

1 teaspoon kosher salt

Pinch of grated nutmeg

1 large egg

8 tablespoons (1 stick) unsalted butter, softened

Pickled Cherries (page 223)

Grilled bread, for serving

1 In a small saucepan over medium heat, simmer the orange juice, Sauternes, shallot, and garlic until reduced by half, about 10 minutes. Strain and then refrigerate to cool.

2 Preheat the oven to 300°F.

3 Put the liver, salt, nutmeg, and chilled orange juice reduction in a blender. Puree on medium speed until smooth. With the blender running, add the egg followed by the softened butter. (If you prefer the mousse extra silky, pass it through a fine-mesh sieve at this point.)

4 Fill each of five (4-ounce) Mason jar three-quarters full with mousse. Wrap the tops of the jars tightly with aluminum foil and put in an 8 by 8-inch baking pan. Fill the baking pan with enough warm water so that it comes up to the middle of the jars.

5 Bake the mousse for 20 minutes. At this point, the mousse should no longer be liquid but slightly firm in the center. Remove from the oven, take the jars out of the water bath, and refrigerate until chilled, at least 5 hours and up to 3 days.

6 To serve, remove the aluminum foil, top each jar with some pickled cherries, and serve with grilled bread.

SPICY WILD BOAR SAUSAGE WITH CILANTRO & LIME

Makes
4
pounds

Occasionally, I will come across some wild boar meat. It's really an amazing treat—think pork with a punch! If I have access to the leg, I normally prepare it like Smoked Ham (page 78). But if I score some wild boar shoulder, I whip up a batch of this killer spicy sausage. This recipe really packs a wallop, so it might be a good idea to crack a cold one before the first bite. Serve with Orange Salad (page 212) or Grilled-Corn Salad (page 217).

3 pounds trimmed boar shoulder, cut into large dice

1 pound boar fat or pork fatback, cut into large dice

3 tablespoons kosher salt

½ cup chopped fresh cilantro

2 garlic cloves, minced

Grated zest of 2 limes

¼ cup canned chipotles in adobo, pureed with sauce

2 tablespoons cumin seeds, toasted and ground

1 tablespoon freshly ground black pepper

Small pinch of cayenne pepper

½ cup whole milk, cold

½ cup dry white wine, cold

6 feet of hog casing, soaked overnight and rinsed (see page 35), optional

1 Combine the boar, fat, salt, cilantro, garlic, lime zest, chipotles, cumin, black pepper, and cayenne in a gallon-sized zip-top bag, turn to coat, and refrigerate overnight.

2 Thoroughly chill all the sausage-grinding equipment, the mixing bowl, and the paddle attachment. Grind the chilled meat mixture through the small die into the chilled mixing bowl. Using the paddle attachment, mix in the milk and wine. Refrigerate until ready to use or for up to 1 week.

3 Stuff this sausage filling into a hog casing (see page 36) and poach in simmering water or grill until the sausage reaches an internal temperature of 160°F; form into patties and pan-roast until browned and cooked through; or leave it loose to crumble into other recipes.

PHEASANT CHILI, AUSTIN-STYLE

As a Midwesterner, I always assumed chili had to have beans. It wasn't until I was at culinary school that I learned the truth. Stewart Scruggs, a big man from Austin, Texas, brought a batch of his chili to watch some Sunday football. And you know what? There wasn't a bean in sight! It also was burn-your-hair-off spicy, which might explain why I soon began to lose my own curly locks. Thanks a lot, Stewart! Regardless, I couldn't stop eating this chili then, and I can't stop making it now.

2 tablespoons olive oil

3 pounds coarsely ground pheasant or chicken, preferably dark meat

Kosher salt

1 large red onion, chopped

3 garlic cloves, sliced

2 red bell peppers, diced

¼ cup cayenne pepper

¼ cup cumin seeds, toasted and ground

1 tablespoon coriander seeds, toasted and ground

1 tablespoon smoked paprika

1 tablespoon tomato paste

2 (12-ounce) bottles of beer, preferably IPA-style

2 (7-ounce) cans chipotles in adobo, pureed with sauce

1 habanero chile, slit down the side

1 Put a large Dutch oven over medium-high heat and add the oil. When the oil is hot, begin browning the meat along with a large pinch of salt. When browned, after about 10 minutes, remove from the pot with a slotted spoon.

2 To the same pot, add the onion, garlic, bell peppers, and another pinch of salt. Cook until aromatic, but not caramelized, 3 to 5 minutes. Add the cayenne, cumin, coriander, and paprika and cook for 30 seconds. Add the tomato paste and cook, stirring, for 30 seconds.

3 Deglaze the pot with the beer, being sure to scrape up the browned bits with a wooden spoon. Let simmer until reduced by one-third. Return the meat to the pot along with the chipotles and habanero, stirring to incorporate. Simmer over low heat, stirring occasionally, for about 2 hours, or until it reaches a thick, hearty consistency.

4 Remove the habanero before serving the chili with your favorite garnishes.

SMOKY GRILLED SQUAB BREASTS

Here in Cleveland, we tend to grill year-round—we're hearty like that. But for those of you who stow the grill at the sight of the first flake of snow, make this recipe one of your last before doing so. This dish is a great way to start a late-autumn feast. The squab is just as good served room-temperature as it is warm, so it's okay to do the grilling a little bit ahead of time. This technique works equally well with chicken, duck, and pheasant; just increase the smoking time to 45 minutes. Serve with Apple & Celery Root Salad (page 209).

8 squab breasts

Kosher salt

2 tablespoons Dijon mustard

1 teaspoon sherry vinegar

1 teaspoon smoked paprika

1 teaspoon coriander seeds, toasted and cracked

1 garlic clove, minced

1 shallot, minced

1 Liberally season the squab breasts with salt. Put the squab in a large zip-top bag, add the mustard, vinegar, paprika, coriander, garlic, and shallot, give it all a good shake so that the squab is well coated; and refrigerate for at least 3 hours or overnight.

2 Soak apple-wood chips in water for at least 30 minutes. Heat one side of a charcoal or gas grill to low heat (200° to 250°F). (For this technique, do not allow the squab to come to room temperature before smoking, as it would cook too fast.)

3 Put the soaked apple-wood chips over the coals (or in a perforated aluminum foil pouch if using a gas grill). Remove the squab from the marinade, shaking off any excess; reserve the marinade for basting. Put the squab breasts skin-side-up on the unheated side of the grill. Cover the grill and adjust the vents to maintain 250°F. Smoke the squab for 20 minutes.

4 Uncover the grill and raise the heat to medium-high. Liberally baste the squab with the reserved marinade. Flip the squab so it is skin-side-down and put it on the heated side of the grill. Cook for 2 to 3 minutes, until the skin gets crisp and the meat reaches 130°F.

5 Remove from the heat and allow the squab to rest for 5 minutes before slicing the breasts.

GRILLED QUAIL WITH CITRUS GLAZE

This sweet-tart quail recipe is not only particularly tasty, but it's also extremely versatile, appropriate for anything from a backyard barbecue to a more formal feast. (To make this dish a bit more upscale, pair it with Shaved Asparagus Salad, page 220.) Better yet, it's super quick to make, meaning us cooks get to spend more time with our guests than with our grills. Once you have all your ingredients prepped, you can literally have the dish ready to go in under 10 minutes. Sweet!

8 semi-boneless quail

Kosher salt

Grated zest and juice of 2 oranges

2 tablespoons sherry vinegar

2 tablespoons honey

1 tablespoon grainy mustard

1 garlic clove, minced

1 jalapeño, seeded and minced

Extra-virgin olive oil, for drizzling

2 tablespoons chopped fresh tarragon

1 Heat a charcoal or gas grill to medium-high.

2 Liberally season the quail with salt.

3 In a small saucepan on the grill, whisk together the orange zest and juice, sherry vinegar, honey, mustard, garlic, and jalapeño.

4 Drizzle the quail with a little olive oil and put on the grill. Using a pastry brush, liberally baste the quail with the heated citrus glaze. Cook for 2 to 4 minutes per side, basting the entire time, until the glaze is slightly charred and the quail are cooked through. Remove the quail from the grill and let rest for 2 minutes.

5 Bring the remaining citrus glaze to a boil.

6 To serve, split each quail, drizzle with olive oil and the remaining citrus glaze, and top with the chopped tarragon.

DUCK PAPRIKASH

Growing up, I used to love going to my friend Todd Krupa's house for paprikash night. It wasn't a dish we ever ate at home, so being invited over was always a special treat. Mrs. K. is a great cook, and her paprikash still ranks up there with the best I've ever had. Years later, Tim Bando, a good friend who also is a chef, put duck paprikash on the menu at one of his restaurants. Tasting it immediately brought me back to my childhood. This recipe is the best of both worlds, combining Bando's duck twist with Mrs. K's killer dumplings and sauce.

DUCK

2 tablespoons smoked spicy paprika

1 tablespoon sweet paprika

1 tablespoon kosher salt

1 (3-pound) whole duck

1 small red onion, cut in half

2 garlic cloves

1 dried chipotle chile

4 sprigs of fresh thyme

DUMPLINGS

1 cup whole milk

½ cup duck fat or unsalted butter

Kosher salt

½ teaspoon freshly ground black pepper

½ teaspoon grated nutmeg

1 cup all-purpose flour

3 large eggs

1 To prepare the duck, mix the smoked paprika, sweet paprika, and kosher salt. Rub this mixture all over the inside and outside of the duck and refrigerate uncovered overnight.

2 Preheat the oven to 450°F.

3 Stuff the cavity of duck with the onion halves, garlic cloves, chipotle pepper, and thyme. Put the duck on a rack in a roasting pan and roast for 20 minutes. Reduce the oven temperature to 325°F and roast for 1 hour, or until the thigh registers 160°F.

4 Remove the duck from the oven and let rest for 30 minutes. Reserve ½ cup plus 2 tablespoons of the duck fat in the roasting pan to make the dumplings and paprika sauce.

5 While the duck is resting, make the dumplings: In a medium saucepan over medium-high heat, bring the milk and fat to a simmer. Add ½ teaspoon salt, pepper, and nutmeg. Remove the pan from the heat and add the flour, stirring with a heavy wooden spoon until the flour has absorbed all of the milk and the resulting dough pulls away from the sides of the pan. Add the eggs, one at a time, stirring each until it is fully incorporated into the dough.

6 Bring a large pot of salted water to a boil. Drop the dough by the tablespoonful into the boiling water and cook for a couple of minutes, until the dumplings float.

PAPRIKA SAUCE

2 tablespoons duck fat

1 medium red onion, thinly sliced

1 garlic clove, minced

1 tablespoon sweet paprika

2 tablespoons all-purpose flour

1 quart chicken broth, preferably homemade (page 163), hot

1 cup sour cream

7 Meanwhile, make the sauce: In a medium saucepan over medium heat, warm the duck fat. Add the onion and garlic and cook for 2 minutes. Add the paprika and cook for 30 seconds. Add the flour, stirring with a wooden spoon. Cook, stirring, for 2 minutes. Slowly add the hot chicken broth, whisking the entire time to fully incorporate it until smooth. Whisk in the sour cream.

8 Drain the dumplings and add them to the sauce.

9 To serve, cut the duck into 8 pieces and serve with the dumplings and sauce.

VENISON SLOPPY JOES

If you can't tell, I love sloppy joes. When you've been a tortured Cleveland Browns fan for forty-plus years like me, you can never have too much comfort food! This version is meaty and chunky and works great with game. Serve this messy dish with a lot of napkins—or just wear something you don't mind getting dirty, like a Pittsburgh Steelers jersey!

3 tablespoons olive oil

4 pounds venison meat from the leg, shoulder, and/or shank, cut into 1-inch cubes

Kosher salt

2 cups small-diced red onion

4 garlic cloves, minced

1 tablespoon chipotle powder

2 teaspoons cayenne pepper

2 teaspoons smoked paprika

2 teaspoons cumin seeds, toasted and ground

2 teaspoons coriander seeds, toasted and ground

1 teaspoon ground cinnamon

1 teaspoon ground allspice

2 tablespoons tomato paste

1 (750 ml) bottle dry red wine

6 tablespoons sherry vinegar

2 tablespoons Dijon mustard

2 tablespoons Sriracha sauce

½ cup packed light brown sugar

1 (24-ounce) can crushed San Marzano tomatoes, with their juice

¼ cup chopped fresh oregano

1 tablespoon granulated sugar

10 to 12 soft buns

1 Put a large Dutch oven over medium-high heat. Add the olive oil to the pot and let it get hot. Pat the venison meat dry and season liberally with salt. Begin browning the meat, about 2 minutes per side. You may need to do this in batches so as not to crowd the pot. When browned on all sides, remove the meat from the pot with a slotted spoon and set aside.

2 Reduce the heat to medium-low, add the onion and garlic along with a pinch of salt, and cook for 2 minutes. Add the chipotle powder, cayenne, paprika, cumin, coriander, cinnamon, and allspice and cook for 2 minutes. Add the tomato paste and cook, stirring, for 2 minutes.

3 Add the red wine, being sure to scrape up the browned bits on the bottom of the pot with a wooden spoon. Once it has reduced by half, about 5 minutes, add the vinegar, Dijon, Sriracha, and brown sugar and simmer until the sugar is dissolved, 2 to 3 minutes. Add the tomatoes and their juice and bring to a simmer.

4 Return the meat to the pot and add the oregano and granulated sugar and simmer until the meat is tender, 3 to 4 hours. If the sauce still is a little loose, continue simmering until it reaches optimum sloppy joe consistency! Serve on buns.

VENISON STEW

Even for us hearty Cleveland folk, there are some winter days that make leaving home feel like cruel and unusual punishment. If we're lucky enough for some of those days to be Sundays, this is the dish that should be simmering all afternoon long on the stovetop. This one-pot Sunday supper will fill your entire house with a heartwarming and soul-satisfying aroma. And since it was you who did all the shopping and cooking, it's okay to make your family and friends leave *their* house to come to yours.

2 tablespoons olive oil

4 pounds venison shoulder or stew meat, cut into 2-inch cubes

Kosher salt

4 red red onions, cut into large dice

2 jalapeños, cut into rings

6 garlic cloves, sliced

1 teaspoon caraway seeds

1 tablespoon sweet paprika

1 tablespoon smoked paprika

1 tablespoon tomato paste

4 (12-ounce) bottles of dark beer

1 pound medium red-skinned potatoes, halved

1 pound medium turnips, peeled and quartered

1 cup sour cream

6 scallions, white and green parts, thinly sliced

1 Put a large Dutch oven over medium-high heat. Add the olive oil to the pot and let it get hot. Pat the venison meat dry and season liberally with salt. Begin browning the meat, about 2 minutes per side. You may need to do this in batches so as not to crowd the pot. Remove to a plate as the meat is browned.

2 To the same pot, add the onions and cook for 3 to 5 minutes, until translucent and aromatic. Add the jalapeños and garlic and cook for about 2 minutes. Add the caraway seeds and sweet and smoked paprika and cook for 1 minute. Add the tomato paste and cook, stirring, for 2 minutes.

3 Deglaze the pot with 1 cup water, scraping up the browned bits on the bottom of the pot with a wooden spoon. Return all of the browned meat to the pot. Add the beer, and bring to a simmer. Cook for 2 hours, occasionally skimming off the fat that rises to the top.

4 Add the potatoes and turnips and simmer for 1 hour, or until the meat, potatoes, and turnips are all tender.

5 Garnish bowls with a dollop of sour cream and a sprinkle of scallions.

MUSTARD-GRILLED ELK CHOPS

The following preparation works really well for grilling elk chops—and also for beef or venison chops and steaks. Thanks to a brushing with a mustard–brown sugar mixture, the chops develop a beautiful crust from the caramelization that takes place on the grill. Pair these meaty, mouth-watering chops with a refreshing arugula salad.

6 elk chops

Kosher salt

6 tablespoons Dijon mustard

¼ cup Roasted Garlic with Parsley & Lemon (page 243)

2 tablespoons packed light brown sugar

2 teaspoons freshly ground black pepper

2 teaspoons freshly ground pink pepper

2 tablespoons chopped fresh rosemary

2 tablespoons olive oil

1 Season both sides of the elk chops liberally with salt. Whisk together the mustard, roasted garlic, and brown sugar. In a separate bowl, mix together the black pepper, pink pepper, and rosemary. Brush the chops with the mustard mixture and then liberally season them with the pepper mixture. Set the chops aside to allow them to reach room temperature for 30 minutes before grilling.

2 Heat a charcoal or gas grill to medium-high.

3 Drizzle the chops with the olive oil and put them on the grill. Cook for about 7 minutes per side, or until they reach medium-rare. Don't fiddle with the chops too much, as you want them to develop a nice crust.

4 Remove the chops from the grill and let rest for 5 minutes before serving.

BACON-WRAPPED RABBIT LEGS

Come fall, we always have rabbit on the menu at Lola. Over the years, we have done a million different versions. This one was dreamed up by Derek Clayton, our corporate chef and fearless kitchen leader. It may look like a bit of a project (in fact, get your butcher to debone the legs, if you can), but the end result makes it all more than worth it. If you haven't tried rabbit yet, this recipe will likely turn you into a fan. The mildly flavored legs taste better than chicken and even better when basted with bacon. Serve these with Sherla's Southern Greens (page 237) for an extra bacon boost.

6 rabbit legs

Kosher salt and freshly ground black pepper

30 strips of bacon, each ⅛ inch thick

2 tablespoons olive oil

1 Dry the rabbit legs with paper towels. Arrange the legs on a work surface flesh-side-up. Make a cut at the knee joint of each leg to pop out the main bone. Then cut out the joint holding the bone in place as well as any surrounding cartilage. Once the bone and joint have been removed, the meat should lie flat as though it's butterflied.

2 Double up a large piece of plastic wrap a few times to create a thicker piece. Put one rabbit leg flesh-side-up on one half of the plastic wrap, fold the remaining plastic wrap up over it to enclose, and then pound the meat with a mallet to an ⅛-inch thickness. This helps break down any tendons and acts as a tenderizer. Repeat one by one with the remaining legs.

3 Trim the meat down to 6 by 4-inch rectangles. (Reserve the trimmings for later use in sausage or stock.) Season both sides with salt and pepper. Roll each leg up into a tight log and set aside.

4 Lay out 5 pieces of bacon, slightly overlapping them like roof shingles. Trim the bacon so it measures 8 inches long. Put one rabbit log at one end of the bacon strips and roll it to form a tight package. Repeat with the remaining bacon and rabbit pieces. Wrap each piece tightly in plastic wrap, twisting the ends to form a tight package. Refrigerate for at least 30 minutes and up to 2 days.

5 Preheat the oven to 400°F.

6 Remove the plastic wrap and tie each rabbit package with kitchen twine so it holds its shape and the bacon stays in place.

(RECIPE CONTINUES)

7 Heat a large ovenproof sauté pan over medium-high heat and add the olive oil. When the oil is hot, add the rabbit and lightly brown on all sides, about 1 minute per side. Transfer the pan to the oven for 3 to 4 minutes, then give the pieces a quarter turn in the pan so that a new side is exposed to the heat, and cook for 3 to 4 minutes. Repeat this process until the rabbit is cooked through, for a total cook time of 12 to 15 minutes.

8 Remove the pan from the oven, baste the meat with the rendered bacon fat in the pan, and then remove it to a plate to rest for 5 minutes. Remove the kitchen twine, slice the meat, and serve.

BRAISED RABBIT THIGHS WITH PRUNES & MACADAMIA NUTS

I love rabbit; it's a shame that it is such an underutilized, underappreciated meat. Not only is it super tasty, but it is also quite healthy. At Lola, rabbit has always been a very good seller for us. I know that some people can't get past the whole cute bunny thing, but, come on! Cows and pigs are pretty darn cute, too, and that doesn't stop us from enjoying *them* for dinner!

Kosher salt

½ teaspoon ground cinnamon

½ teaspoon coriander seeds, toasted and ground

⅛ teaspoon ground juniper berry

12 rabbit thighs or legs

¼ cup olive oil

All-purpose flour, for dredging

2 cups medium-diced red onion

4 garlic cloves, minced

2 cups diced peeled celery root

1 (750 ml) bottle dry red wine

2 cups pitted prunes, roughly chopped

2 star anise

1 ham hock

About 5 cups chicken broth, preferably homemade (page 163)

1 cup macadamia nuts, toasted and chopped

1 In a gallon-sized zip-top bag, mix together ¼ cup salt, the cinnamon, coriander, and the juniper. Add the rabbit thighs or legs, toss to coat with this mixture, and refrigerate overnight.

2 Preheat the oven to 325°F.

3 Put a large Dutch oven over medium-high heat and add the olive oil. Dredge the rabbit pieces with flour, shaking off any excess, and begin adding them to the pot, working in batches if necessary. Brown for 3 to 5 minutes per side, until golden brown. Remove the rabbit from the pot and reduce the heat to medium.

4 To the same pot, add the onion and a pinch of salt and slowly caramelize for about 5 minutes. Add the garlic and celery root and cook for 2 minutes. Deglaze the pot with the red wine, scraping up the browned bits from the bottom of the pot with a wooden spoon. When the wine comes to a simmer, return the rabbit to the pot. Add the prunes, star anise, ham hock, and enough broth to cover the rabbit. Bring to a simmer and check the braising liquid for seasoning. You may want to add some salt. Cover the pot and put in the oven for 4 to 5 hours, until the meat is really tender.

5 Remove from the oven, top with the macadamia nuts, and serve.

BRAISING

Braising is one of my favorite methods of cooking. It magically transforms cheap cuts of meat like bellies, shanks, and necks into quivering morsels of melt-in-your-mouth goodness. Despite the lengthy amount of time it takes to properly make a braised dish, the technique is not complicated. Follow these straightforward steps and you, too, will be braising like a pro:

1 Brown the meat well. Do this by getting your pan and fat good and hot, paper-towel-drying the meat before adding it to the pan, not crowding the pan with too many pieces at a time, *and leaving the meat alone!* Flip only when the meat is brown and releases easily from the bottom of the pan.

2 Deglaze the pan. After all of the meat is browned and pulled from the pan, and after the aromatics (celery, carrot, onion, etc.) have had a chance to cook, add some liquid (wine, water, broth, etc.). Now, scrape up all the brown goodies from the bottom of the pan with a wooden spoon. This is where all the flavor is hiding.

3 Taste the liquid. Is it properly seasoned? If not, how do you think the meat will taste? Adjust as needed.

4 The meat should not be completely submerged in the liquid—this isn't a stew. There should be just enough liquid to come three-quarters of the way up the meat, with the fattiest part of the cut peeking out.

5 Baste the meat every 30 minutes or so to keep that exposed portion moist and help develop a nice crust.

6 I always braise the day before serving. This way I can strain the sauce, pour it back over the meat, and chill it all overnight. Not only does the meat absorb all those great flavors from the sauce, but all the fat settles and congeals on the top, making it super easy to discard. Reheat gently, and serve!

SIDES

*B*eyond sourcing good meat and cooking it properly, the biggest thing that will set your dishes apart from average ones is the sides. This is where you really get to see the creativity of a chef or home cook. Think of the sides as the accessories to a great outfit—they are the perfect opportunity to personalize your plates.

My general rule for sides is this: The richer the meat, the more texture and acidity I want in the side to balance the dish. Serve soft and unctuous meats, like Braised Veal Short Ribs (page 52), with something crunchy and bright, like Gremolata (page 228) or Giardinera (page 225). A perfect example of this is the pairing of citrusy Grapefruit Salad (page 214) with hearty Braised Lamb Necks (page 127).

Sides are also the dishes that are the easiest to tailor to the seasons. If it's the middle of August, nobody wants to dig into a pile of steaming mashed potatoes. Think Shaved Asparagus Salad (page 220) or Pickled Cherries (page 223). Likewise, if it's the dead of winter, go for Brussels sprouts over tomatoes. While I love the combo of Veal Sirloin Minute Steaks (page 23) with Tomato Salad with Red Onion & Dill (page 207), when I make this in fall or winter, I top it instead with Apple & Celery Root Salad (page 209) or Orange Salad (page 212). Of course, if you regularly shop at farmers' markets, the ingredients on offer are guaranteed to be seasonal and you can't go wrong.

TOMATO SALAD WITH
RED ONION & DILL

This is summer in a salad. Use an assortment of various shapes, sizes, and colors of heirloom tomatoes for the best flavor and presentation. Fresh dill really wakes this salad up. It's great on its own or with any steak, especially a nice fatty rib eye or Veal Sirloin Minute Steaks (page 23).

1 cup thinly shaved red onion

1 pound heirloom tomatoes

1 garlic clove, minced

Kosher salt

¼ cup red wine vinegar

½ cup extra-virgin olive oil

1 red bell pepper, seeded and cut into 1-inch chunks

1 cup thinly sliced cucumber

¼ cup chopped fresh dill

¼ cup chopped fresh mint

Freshly ground black pepper

1 Soak the onion in ice water for 10 minutes. Drain and pat dry.

2 Cut the tomatoes into bite-sized chunks.

3 In a large bowl, combine the garlic, a pinch of salt, and the vinegar. Whisk in the olive oil in a slow stream. Add the onion, bell pepper, cucumber, dill, and mint. Let marinate for 15 to 20 minutes.

4 Add the tomatoes and toss gently to combine. Season with salt and black pepper to taste. Put on a large platter and serve immediately.

APPLE & CELERY ROOT SALAD

This crunchy, refreshing salad is a great topper for pork. I especially like it with pig trotters (see page 85).

2 Granny Smith apples

1 medium celery root, peeled and cored

¼ cup cider vinegar

Kosher salt

1 shallot, minced

2 tablespoons grainy mustard

½ cup extra-virgin olive oil

2 tablespoons chopped fresh tarragon

1 cup watercress, tough stems trimmed

1 Slice the apples and celery root into long, thin matchsticks by hand or with the aid of a mandoline. Put in a nonreactive bowl and toss with the vinegar and a large pinch of salt.

2 In a small bowl, combine the shallot and a good pinch of salt. Whisk in the mustard, olive oil, and tarragon. Pour the dressing over the apples and celery root and toss to combine. Let this mixture sit for about 20 minutes.

3 When ready to serve, toss in the watercress.

HONEY NECTARINES

I love eating ripe stone fruit like peaches and nectarines fresh from the farmer's market. But something truly special happens when the fruit is heated. To me, this sauce screams summer, especially with the last-minute addition of fresh mint. It's great with grilled meats but also spooned over vanilla bean ice cream!

¾ cup dry rosé or white wine

Juice of 3 limes

¼ cup honey

1 shallot, minced

12 nectarines, pitted and quartered

3 tablespoons chopped fresh mint

3 tablespoons pine nuts, toasted

1 Bring the wine, lime juice, honey, and shallot to a simmer in a small non-reactive saucepan over medium heat. Add the nectarines and cook until the mixture is syrupy, about 20 minutes.

2 Gently stir in the mint and pine nuts. Serve hot or at room temperature.

ORANGE SALAD

Bright, healthy, and pleasantly crunchy, this lively citrus salad is a great substitute for a boring green salad. Serve it as a starter course or pair it with roasted meats like Coriander-and-Orange-Roasted Chicken (page 148) or Grilled Lamb Chops with Lavender Salt (page 119).

3 oranges, segmented (see page 214), with their juice

½ cup slivered almonds, toasted

2 cups watercress, tough stems trimmed

Kosher salt and freshly ground black pepper

¼ cup extra-virgin olive oil

In a medium bowl, toss to combine the orange segments with their juice, the almonds, and watercress. Season with salt and pepper, drizzle with the olive oil, and toss again to combine.

COLESLAW

If you haven't been putting coleslaw on hot dogs, sausages, and hamburgers, you are totally missing out! Our pastrami and coleslaw-topped Fat Doug Burger (page 44) at B Spot is the most popular sandwich on the menu. Napa cabbage and champagne vinegar make this version nice and crisp.

½ head Napa cabbage, shredded

½ garlic clove, minced

1 cup thinly sliced red onion

½ jalapeño, seeds and ribs removed, minced

3 tablespoons champagne vinegar

2 tablespoons mayonnaise

1 tablespoon Dijon mustard

1 tablespoon spicy mustard

1 tablespoon Worcestershire sauce

1 tablespoon sugar

1½ teaspoons kosher salt

Mix all of the ingredients together in a large bowl, cover, and refrigerate for 1 hour before serving.

GRAPEFRUIT SALAD

This wonderful mix of citrus, cheese, olives, and herbs is one that can be tweaked in countless ways by swapping out various components. This particular combination is inspired by Greece, and it goes amazingly well with Braised Lamb Necks (page 127).

2 grapefruits

1 cup crumbled feta cheese, preferably Greek

¼ cup pitted Kalamata olives

2 cups fresh flat-leaf parsley leaves

Grated zest and juice of 2 lemons

¼ cup extra-virgin olive oil

1 Slice off the tops and bottoms of the grapefruits, exposing some of the fruit. Working your way around each fruit, slice off the peel, removing the white pith and a sliver of fruit with each slice, until you have completely peeled the grapefruit and no pith remains. Working over a large bowl to catch the juice, use a paring knife to slice between the membranes to free each grapefruit segment. Drop the segments into the bowl, checking for pits and removing them once you have finished.

2 Add the feta, olives, and parsley leaves to the grapefruit segments.

3 In a small bowl, whisk together the lemon zest and juice and the olive oil. Pour the vinaigrette over the grapefruit mixture and gently toss to combine.

Serves
6 *to* **8**

SHAVED BRUSSELS SPROUTS

Like asparagus, Brussels sprouts don't have to be cooked to be eaten, even if we rarely think of them that way. The key to this recipe, which was inspired by one of my best friends and favorite chefs, Jonathan Waxman, is to shave the sprouts paper-thin. This is great on its own or paired with rich braises like the Braised Pork Shanks (page 94).

1 shallot, minced

1 garlic clove, minced

2 tablespoons caraway seeds, toasted

1 tablespoon grainy mustard

¼ cup cider vinegar

½ cup extra-virgin olive oil

Kosher salt

1 pound Brussels sprouts, shaved paper-thin

1 To make the vinaigrette, whisk together the shallot, garlic, caraway seeds, mustard, vinegar, and olive oil. Season with salt to taste.

2 Toss the shaved sprouts with the dressing to coat. Serve immediately.

GRILLED-CORN SALAD

Ohio sweet corn really is the best on Earth. Maybe because it's super fresh, but I can't seem to get enough of the candy-sweet kernels come summertime. Grilling corn adds a whole new dimension that makes it go great with grilled items like sausage and BBQ Chicken Legs (page 158).

4 ears of corn

Kosher salt

1 anchovy, minced

1 garlic clove, minced

1 jalapeño, seeds and ribs removed, minced

Grated zest and juice of 3 limes

½ cup extra-virgin olive oil

1 ripe Hass avocado, peeled and diced

1 cup halved cherry tomatoes

6 scallions, white and green parts, thinly sliced

¾ cup chopped fresh cilantro

1 Soak the ears of corn in their husks overnight in salted water.

2 Heat a charcoal or gas grill to medium-low.

3 Put the soaked ears, still in their husks, on the grill and close the lid. Cook for 20 minutes.

4 Meanwhile, in a large bowl, combine the anchovy, garlic, jalapeño, and a large pinch of salt. Add the lime zest and juice and whisk in the olive oil. Add the avocado, tomatoes, scallions, and cilantro and gently toss.

5 Remove the corn from the grill and let it cool enough so that you can handle it. Peel off and discard the husks. Working over the salad bowl to catch any juices, cut the kernels from the cobs and then add them to the salad. Toss to combine and taste and adjust for seasoning. You may need to add some additional salt.

FETA & CUCUMBER SALAD

I love this salad with all sorts of lamb and chicken dishes, but it's especially tasty with Grilled Lamb Chops with Lavender Salt (page 119), Leg of Lamb Souvlaki (page 128), and Grilled Marinated Chicken Breasts (page 157).

3 cucumbers, unpeeled

Kosher salt

1 garlic clove, minced

1 shallot, minced

1 jalapeño, seeded and minced

2 tablespoons fresh oregano leaves

Grated zest and juice of 2 lemons

¼ cup extra-virgin olive oil

1 cup crumbled feta cheese

1 Slice the cucumbers as thinly as you can. A mandoline or vegetable slicer will make quick work of it. In a nonreactive bowl, toss the cucumbers with a large pinch of salt.

2 In a small bowl, whisk together the garlic, shallot, jalapeño, oregano, a pinch of salt, the lemon zest and juice, and then the olive oil.

3 Drain off and discard any water that the cucumbers have released. Add the dressing and toss to combine. Just before serving, toss in the feta.

SHAVED ASPARAGUS SALAD

Serves
4

Asparagus doesn't need to be steamed to be enjoyed, as proven by this simple salad. It's best to give the dressing a few minutes to soften the raw asparagus before serving. The addition of chopped hazelnuts adds a layer of crunch. Try pairing it with Brick-Grilled Chicken (page 161) or Grilled Lamb Chops with Lavender Salt (page 119).

1 large bunch thick green asparagus (2 pounds), trimmed

1 (1½-ounce) block Pecorino Romano cheese

Kosher salt

Grated zest and juice of 1 orange, plus 2 oranges, segmented (see page 214)

1½ tablespoons chopped fresh chives

2 teaspoons white wine vinegar

¼ cup extra-virgin olive oil

2 tablespoons coarsely chopped hazelnuts, toasted

1 Shave the asparagus with a vegetable peeler to create long ribbons. Do the same with the Pecorino Romano cheese to create shavings. In a large non-reactive bowl, toss together the asparagus, cheese, and a large pinch of salt.

2 In a small bowl, whisk together the orange zest and juice, the chives, and vinegar. Whisk in the olive oil. Pour the dressing over the asparagus and let sit until the asparagus is slightly wilted, about 5 minutes.

3 Toss in the hazelnuts and orange segments and serve.

PICKLED SHALLOTS

The bright acidity and mellow sweetness of these shallots make them the perfect counter-balance to rich dishes like Roasted Bone Marrow (page 49) or charcuterie. In fact, I don't think I've found anything that this versatile condiment doesn't go great with—that's why I always try to have some on hand.

4 cups thinly sliced shallots

1 cup white wine vinegar

1 cup rice vinegar

2 garlic cloves

½ cup sugar

¼ cup kosher salt

1 teaspoon black peppercorns

1 teaspoon coriander seeds

1 bay leaf, fresh or dried

1 Put the shallots in a nonreactive 1-quart container.

2 In a nonreactive saucepan, bring the remaining ingredients to a simmer, whisking until the sugar and salt are completely dissolved. Remove from the heat and strain the mixture over the shallots, discarding the solids.

3 Put a weighted dish on top of the shallots so they remain fully submerged in the liquid. Allow to cool before transferring to the refrigerator. Stored in the pickling liquid, the shallots will keep in the fridge for up to 1 month.

PICKLED CHERRIES

Pickling fruit might sound odd, but the result is a remarkably complex condiment that combines sweetness, tartness, and a hint of homey spice. The acidity and ripe fruit flavor make this a perfect partner for roasted game and Duck Liver Mousse (page 181).

2 pounds Bing cherries

3 cups red wine vinegar

1½ cups sugar

2 tablespoons kosher salt

2 strips orange zest, removed with a vegetable peeler

1 teaspoon black peppercorns

2 cinnamon sticks

1 tablespoon coriander seeds

1 bay leaf, fresh or dried

1 Prick each cherry with a fork several times and put the cherries in a large nonreactive jar or container.

2 Combine the remaining ingredients in a nonreactive saucepan and bring to a boil. Reduce the heat and simmer for 10 minutes. Remove from the heat and let cool for 10 minutes.

3 Pour the liquid over the cherries (they should be completely covered). When the mixture is completely cool, seal the jar and refrigerate for up to 1 month.

GIARDINIERA

This spicy, fresh, crisp, and tart celery salad is the perfect counterpoint to almost anything rich and meaty. It's the customary condiment for hot Italian beef sandwiches, but it goes just as well with hot dogs, sausages, and Grilled Veal Hearts (page 46).

1 pound celery, peeled and thinly sliced on the bias

1 cup thinly sliced red onion

¼ cup chopped fresh flat-leaf parsley

½ cup thinly sliced jalapeños

2 tablespoons thinly sliced Fresno chile

2 garlic cloves, minced

1 tablespoon coriander seeds, toasted and ground

1 teaspoon ancho chile powder

2 teaspoons kosher salt

1 teaspoon freshly ground black pepper

½ cup red wine vinegar

½ cup extra-virgin olive oil

Mix together all of the ingredients in a large nonreactive bowl or glass jars, cover, and refrigerate for 24 hours before serving.

MUSTARD FRUIT

Another one of my go-to condiments, mustard fruit sets off the sweetness of mulled fruit against the kick of mustard. Use the best grainy mustard you can for the most impressive results. Serve on top of roasted meats or as part of a platter of cheese and cured meats.

1 cup dry red wine

¼ cup red wine vinegar

½ cup sugar

1 teaspoon kosher salt

⅓ cup grainy mustard

½ teaspoon mustard seeds

1 underripe pear, cored
and cut into cubes

1 cup dried tart cherries

1 In a small nonreactive saucepan, combine the wine, vinegar, sugar, and salt and bring to a boil. Stir in the mustard and mustard seeds.

2 Put the pear and cherries in a quart-sized glass jar and pour in the hot liquid. Cover the jar and store in the refrigerator for at least 2 days and up to 1 month.

3 To serve, remove the fruit from the liquid with a slotted spoon.

GREMOLATA

This is the classic condiment for braised veal shanks, but I also pair it with Braised Veal Short Ribs (page 52), a match that works equally well. The lively mix of lemon, herbs, and garlic really perks up hearty stews and other slow-cooked meats.

¾ cup chopped fresh flat-leaf parsley

1 tablespoon grated lemon zest

1 teaspoon fresh lemon juice

2 garlic cloves, minced

¼ teaspoon kosher salt

2 tablespoons extra-virgin olive oil

Combine all of the ingredients in a small bowl, mixing to incorporate. Use immediately.

PEACH & BLUE CHEESE SALAD

I love this salad served right on top of a grilled rib-eye steak or elk chop, but it is also great as a side salad. As for the blue cheese, I'm currently obsessed with smoked ones from Wisconsin, but feel free to use your favorite here.

1 garlic clove, minced

¼ cup red wine vinegar

1 teaspoon Dijon mustard

1 teaspoon honey

¼ cup extra-virgin olive oil, plus more for brushing

6 firm peaches, pitted and quartered

½ cup Marcona almonds

2 cups arugula

1 cup crumbled blue cheese

Kosher salt

1 Heat a charcoal or gas grill to high or preheat the oven to 250°F.

2 In a small bowl, whisk together the garlic, vinegar, mustard, honey, and the ¼ cup olive oil.

3 Brush the peach quarters with olive oil. Grill them for 1 minute per side, or warm them in the oven for 2 minutes.

4 Gently combine the warm peaches, almonds, arugula, and blue cheese in a large bowl. Add the dressing and toss to combine. Season with salt to taste.

SEARED WILD MUSHROOMS

The key to getting a good sear on mushrooms is not to crowd the pan and to take your time. The fresh tarragon in this recipe makes all the difference. Seared mushrooms are great on grilled steaks and chops, of course, but also with Derek's Sweetbreads (page 56).

1 pound wild mushrooms, preferably a mix of oyster, lobster, and chanterelle

Olive oil

Kosher salt

Small bunch fresh tarragon

2 shallots, minced

2 garlic cloves, minced

1 teaspoon unsalted butter

1 Slice the oyster mushrooms into ¼-inch-thick pieces. Slice the lobster mushrooms into ⅛-inch-thick pieces. Quarter or halve the chanterelles lengthwise to form pieces of a similar size.

2 Heat a large sauté pan over medium-high heat for 20 to 30 seconds. Glaze the bottom of the pan with oil. Working in batches, begin browning the mushrooms in the pan, taking care not to overcrowd the pan. When the mushrooms start to get a nice sear, sprinkle them with salt and add a few sprigs of tarragon. When the mushrooms are golden brown on all sides, about 6 minutes, remove from the pan and set aside. Repeat with any remaining mushrooms.

3 Add the shallots and garlic to the same pan along with a sprinkle of salt. Cook over medium heat for about 1 minute. Return all of the mushrooms to the pan and add the butter. When the butter has melted and coated the mushrooms, they are ready to serve.

BRAISED CABBAGE

There is no shortage of cabbage recipes in Cleveland, thanks to our Eastern European roots. But you don't have to be a Midwesterner to love the versatility of this humble vegetable. It's great raw, pickled, braised, and roasted. This version goes great with pork and Stuffed Brisket (page 50).

1 cup diced bacon

1 cup thinly sliced yellow onion

Kosher salt

2 heads Savoy cabbage, thinly sliced

1 (12-ounce) bottle of IPA-style beer

2 tablespoons brown mustard (my favorite is Bertman Ball Park), or more to taste

2 tablespoons cider vinegar, or more to taste

2 tablespoons chopped fresh flat-leaf parsley

½ cup chopped fresh chives

1 Heat a large Dutch oven over medium-high heat. Add the bacon and cook until crisp, about 5 minutes. Add the onion along with a pinch of salt and cook until translucent, 3 to 5 minutes. Add the cabbage and beer along with another large pinch of salt, cover, and cook until the cabbage is wilted, but still slightly crisp, 15 minutes.

2 Stir in the mustard and vinegar and taste for seasoning. You might want to add some additional salt, mustard, and/or vinegar at this time. Remove the cabbage from the heat, stir in the parsley and chives, and serve.

HORSERADISH BEETS

By combining beets with horseradish root, you end up with an earthy-sweet heat that is unforgettable. I prefer using golden beets for this because they have a slightly milder flavor than the more common red variety. Serve this with Prime Rib (page 29) or any other rich and hearty meat.

4 large golden beets

4 ounces fresh horseradish

¼ cup sherry vinegar

2 tablespoons extra-virgin olive oil

2 tablespoons Dijon mustard

Grated zest and juice of 1 orange

2 tablespoons honey

Large pinch of kosher salt

1 Peel the beets and horseradish. Using the coarse side of a box grater, grate the beets into a large nonreactive bowl. You should have about 8 cups. Using the fine side of the box grater, grate the horseradish into the bowl with the beets. You should have about 1 cup.

2 Add the vinegar, oil, mustard, orange zest and juice, the honey, and salt. Mix well, cover with plastic wrap, and refrigerate overnight.

3 Remove from the fridge and put in a strainer to remove any excess liquid. Serve at room temperature.

SICILIAN CAULIFLOWER

Oven-roasting cauliflower is one of those wildly simple but utterly transformative cooking methods. This recipe goes a step further by turning roasted cauliflower into a complex salad with myriad flavors and textures. This sweet, sour, and spicy side dish goes well with Smoky Grilled Squab Breasts (page 186) or any game.

1 head cauliflower,
cut into florets

8 tablespoons extra-virgin
olive oil

Kosher salt

½ cup golden raisins

1 cup Marsala wine

Grated zest and juice
of 1 lemon

Grated zest and juice
of 1 orange

1 teaspoon minced white
anchovy

1 teaspoon red pepper flakes

1 teaspoon cumin seeds,
toasted

1 tablespoon honey

4 shallots, minced

1 garlic clove, minced

½ cup pine nuts, toasted

2 tablespoons capers, rinsed

2 tablespoons chopped fresh
flat-leaf parsley

1 Preheat the oven to 400°F.

2 Toss the cauliflower florets with 2 tablespoons of the olive oil and salt. Spread them out on a baking sheet and roast until lightly golden brown, about 20 minutes. Remove from the oven and set aside to cool.

3 Meanwhile, plump the raisins in the Marsala.

4 Whisk together the lemon and orange zests and juices, the anchovy, red pepper flakes, cumin, and honey. Whisk in the remaining 6 tablespoons olive oil.

5 In another bowl, combine the shallots, garlic, and a pinch of salt, and let sit for 5 minutes.

6 Toss together the cauliflower, raisins and Marsala, pine nuts, and capers. Add the shallot mixture to the vinaigrette and pour over the cauliflower. Stir in the parsley and serve.

SHERLA'S SOUTHERN GREENS

Lizzie's mom is from Dalton, Georgia, and she's a great cook. So when I want to make anything with a Southern twist, I go straight to Sherla for advice. Here is my take on her collard greens, where I use a mix of hearty greens. This dish is great as a side to anything pork, but it's also comfortable on a plate alongside spicy fried chicken (see page 151). Remember: When cooking greens, there is a ton of shrinkage. Visualize how much you want to end up with, and multiply that amount by about ten when buying the raw greens.

1 pound Swiss chard

1 pound mustard greens

1 pound kale

1 pound collard greens

1 pound bacon, homemade (page 75) or store-bought slab, diced

2 cups diced red onions

4 garlic cloves, thinly sliced

1 teaspoon red pepper flakes

Kosher salt

6 tablespoons red wine vinegar, or more to taste

1 teaspoon sugar

Sriracha or other hot sauce

1 Roughly chop all the greens (with their ribs intact) into about ½-inch strips. You should get about 8 cups of each.

2 In a large Dutch oven or stockpot over medium heat, cook the bacon until almost crisp, about 5 minutes. Add the onions and cook for 3 minutes. Add the garlic and cook for 1 minute.

3 Add the greens to the pot along with the red pepper flakes and 1 tablespoon salt. Cover the pot, reduce the heat to low, and cook for 10 minutes. Add the vinegar and sugar. Cover and cook for 30 minutes.

4 Remove from the heat and taste for seasoning. Add salt if necessary, or, if you like it more tart, more vinegar. Add a couple of dashes of Sriracha or to taste. Serve hot.

CREAMED LEEKS

People who might not love onions usually fall head over heels for leeks. With their mild onion and garlic flavor, leeks strike a perfect chord. When they are slowly sautéed and combined with cream—as in this recipe—well, the results are magical. And because almost everything is better with a little kick, I add a dash of cayenne. Pair with Derek's Sweetbreads (page 56) or any grilled, roasted, or sautéed meat.

2 tablespoons olive oil

3 cups small-diced leeks, white parts only

Kosher salt

3 garlic cloves, minced

1 large shallot, minced

1 cup heavy cream

¼ teaspoon cayenne pepper

Put a large sauté pan over medium-high heat. When the pan is hot, add the olive oil and leeks along with a pinch of salt. Cook the leeks, stirring occasionally, for 3 minutes, or until softened. Add the garlic and shallot and cook for another minute. Reduce the heat to low and add the cream, cayenne, and ½ teaspoon salt. Simmer the leeks until the cream is slightly reduced and thickened, coating the leeks, about 2 minutes. Check and adjust for seasoning.

SKORDALIA

Skordalia recipes change from region to region throughout Greece. This bread-based version is less common than the typical one made with potato, but I prefer it because it is lighter. Bread also allows the flavors of the garlic and citrus to shine through. If you don't have day-old bread, cube up some fresh bread and bake it in the oven at 350°F for 5 to 10 minutes. Serve with lamb dishes or as a dip for vegetables.

4 cups cubed day-old bread, crusts removed

2 cups whole milk

2 tablespoons canola oil

¾ cup sliced almonds

½ cup sliced shallots

¼ cup sliced garlic

Kosher salt

2 cups extra-virgin olive oil

Juice of 2 lemons

1 Put the bread in a large bowl and cover with the milk, pressing the bread down into the liquid so it's fully immersed.

2 Put a sauté pan over medium-high heat and add the canola oil. When the oil is hot, add the sliced almonds and toast for 2 minutes, or until golden. Remove from the pan and set aside on a plate.

3 In the same sauté pan, combine the shallots, garlic, and a pinch of salt. Cook until fragrant, about 2 minutes. Remove from the heat.

4 Lift the soaked bread out of the milk without wringing it out. Just let the excess milk drain off. Put the bread in a blender, reserving the excess milk to thin out the *skordalia* later if needed. Add to the blender the olive oil, the shallot mixture, the almonds, lemon juice, and salt to taste. Blend until the mixture is a smooth paste. Add some of the reserved milk if the consistency is too pasty. Taste and adjust for seasoning.

SPICY FRIED POTATOES

Serves
4 *to* **6**

I absolutely love these Spanish tapas–inspired potatoes. Like the original, they possess a nice kick of heat, and they work just as well as a starter as they do a side dish. This version is so darn good, you'll never look at French fries the same way again.

2 pounds baby Yukon gold potatoes

Kosher salt

¼ cup olive oil

1 tablespoon smoked paprika

1 tablespoon chipotle powder

3 garlic cloves, smashed and peeled

½ cup mayonnaise

2 tablespoons Sriracha sauce

1 cup rendered fat (I love bacon or duck)

Flaky sea salt, such as Cyprus Flake or Maldon

Grated zest and juice of 2 limes

¼ cup chopped fresh chives

1 Put the potatoes in a pot, cover with heavily salted cold water, and bring to a boil. Cook until tender, about 20 minutes. Drain the potatoes and let cool.

2 In a small sauté pan over medium heat, combine the oil, paprika, chipotle powder, and garlic. Warm for 1 minute, then remove from the heat and discard the garlic. Combine the mayo and Sriracha in a small serving bowl and whisk in the oil mixture.

3 In a large cast-iron skillet, heat the fat to 350°F. The fat should come 1 to 2 inches up the sides of the pan.

4 Smash each potato with the palm of your hand so it is relatively flat, but still holding together. Add the potatoes to the fat and cook for about 3 minutes per side, or until golden brown.

5 Remove the potatoes from the fat with a slotted spoon and put in a large bowl. Sprinkle them with sea salt, the lime zest and juice, and the chives. Serve immediately with the spicy mayo on the side for dipping.

GRAPEFRUIT TABBOULEH

This recipe is a twist on the Lebanese salad made with bulgur wheat and parsley. Here, I add fresh grapefruit segments, which really wake up the salad and anything it touches. If you don't love grapefruit as much as I do, go ahead and substitute oranges.

½ cup bulgur wheat

Kosher salt

Grated zest and juice of 3 lemons

½ cup extra-virgin olive oil, or more if needed

3 cups chopped fresh flat-leaf parsley

¼ cup chopped scallions, white and green parts

½ cup chopped fresh mint

3 grapefruits, segmented (see page 214) and cut into thirds

1 In a small saucepan, bring 2 cups water to a boil over medium heat. Add the bulgur and cook until the bulgur has absorbed all the water and is slightly tender, about 12 minutes. Season with ½ teaspoon salt and set aside to cool.

2 In a small bowl, whisk together the lemon zest and juice and the olive oil.

3 In a large salad bowl, combine the parsley, scallions, mint, and grapefruit. Add the bulgur, pour the dressing over the salad, and toss to combine. Taste and adjust for seasoning. You might need to add more salt or olive oil. If you need more olive oil, add it 1 tablespoon at a time.

ROASTED GARLIC WITH PARSLEY & LEMON

Makes
1
cup

Roasted garlic is amazing—mellow, sweet, and nutty. But this recipe brightens up the normally one-dimensional spread with lemon and fresh herbs. It's a great topper for grilled meats.

1 head garlic

1 tablespoon extra-virgin olive oil

Grated zest and juice of 1 lemon

¼ cup chopped fresh flat-leaf parsley

1 tablespoon chopped fresh oregano

1 teaspoon kosher salt

1 Preheat the oven to 350°F.

2 Slice the head of garlic in half crosswise. Drizzle both sides with the olive oil, combine the halves in a square of aluminum foil, and pinch the corners closed to create a bundle. Roast for about 40 minutes, until the garlic is slightly caramelized.

3 Remove from the oven to cool slightly. Squeeze the cloves out of the papery skins into a small mixing bowl. Mash the garlic with the back of a fork until it starts to form a paste. This will be easier to do while the garlic is still warm. Add the lemon zest and juice, the parsley, oregano, and salt and mix to incorporate. The garlic will keep for up to 1 week covered in the refrigerator.

FREGOLA IN TOMATO SAUCE

Fregola is a rolled pasta from Sardinia that has more than a few similarities with Israeli-style couscous. The small size and shape of this nutty pasta make it a great addition to soups and sides. Try this recipe served alongside any chicken dish.

6 tablespoons olive oil

1 cup medium-diced peeled carrot

1 cup medium-diced yellow onion

1 cup medium-diced peeled turnip

1 cup medium-diced peeled rutabaga

3 garlic cloves, smashed and peeled

3 sprigs fresh thyme

3 bay leaves, preferably fresh

Kosher salt

1 (12-ounce) can San Marzano crushed tomatoes

½ teaspoon red pepper flakes

1 cup fregola

1 cup thinly sliced kale

½ cup freshly grated Parmesan cheese

1 In a large pot, heat the olive oil over medium heat. Add the carrots, onion, turnip, rutabaga, garlic, thyme, and bay leaves along with a large pinch of salt. Cook the vegetables and aromatics until slightly tender, about 10 minutes. Add the tomatoes, 1 cup water, and the red pepper flakes and simmer for 30 minutes.

2 Meanwhile, bring a small saucepan of salted water to a boil. Add the fregola and simmer for 10 minutes. Drain well.

3 Add the fregola and kale to the vegetable mixture and cook for 3 minutes.

4 Pick out the garlic cloves, thyme stems, and bay leaves and discard. Stir in the Parmesan, taste and adjust for seasoning, and serve.

FRESH PAPPARDELLE

Makes
1
pound

I learned this dough recipe from chef Marc Vetri, and it is by far the best pasta dough I have ever used. The double-zero (00) flour is finer than all-purpose, which creates a cooked pasta with a softer, more delicate texture. It is available at most Italian groceries and specialty markets.

1½ cups double-zero (00) flour

9 large egg yolks

1 tablespoon extra-virgin olive oil

2 teaspoons ice water

Rice flour

1 In the bowl of a mixer fitted with the paddle attachment, mix the double zero flour, yolks, olive oil, and ice water on medium speed until the mixture just comes together. Switch to the dough hook. Knead on medium speed until the dough becomes one solid, smooth piece, 4 to 6 minutes.

2 Wrap the dough in plastic and let it rest in the refrigerator for at least 30 minutes or up to 1 week.

3 Set up the pasta machine. Cut the dough into 4 equal pieces. Working with one piece at a time (while keeping the others covered), flatten it in your hands. If the dough feels very dry, dampen the surface with a few drops of water with your fingers or a pastry brush. Starting with the rollers of the pasta machine set to the widest setting, pass the dough through until it becomes pliable, 2 or 3 passes. Repeat with the remaining pieces, keeping each one covered when not working with it. Reduce the roller width by one setting and pass each piece through once. Continue reducing the rollers by one setting and passing the pasta through once with each piece until the dough reaches the desired thickness. For pappardelle, this will be setting 6 or 7.

4 Roll the pasta into cylinders. Using a sharp knife, cut the pasta into ½-inch-wide by 10-inch-long strands. Toss the cut pasta with rice flour to prevent sticking. At this point, the pasta can sit at room temperature covered with parchment paper or a dry kitchen towel for up to half a day. It can also be frozen in zip-top bags for up to a month. There is no need to thaw frozen pasta before cooking.

SOFT POLENTA
WITH AGED CHEDDAR

Polenta just might be the ultimate Italian comfort food, and it's always one of the most popular items at Lola and Lolita. Creamy, cheesy, and delicious, polenta like this will make you forget about mashed potatoes forever. I love it paired with Smoked Pork Chops (page 73).

6 tablespoons (¾ stick) unsalted butter

½ cup minced yellow onion

1 garlic clove, minced

4 cups chicken broth, preferably homemade (page 163)

2 cups polenta, preferably Anson Mills

½ cup shredded aged cheddar

Kosher salt

1 In a 4-quart saucepan over medium heat, melt 2 tablespoons of the butter. Add the onion and garlic and cook until translucent and aromatic, about 5 minutes. Add the broth and bring to a simmer. Slowly whisk in the polenta and reduce the heat to low. Cook, stirring frequently, for 2 hours, until it reaches the consistency of smooth mashed potatoes.

2 Remove from the heat and whisk in the cheddar and the remaining 4 tablespoons butter. Season to taste with salt. Serve hot.

CORN TORTILLAS

I know the temptation is to buy store-bought corn tortillas. But as with bread, the difference between fresh and packaged is night and day. Made with lard, these 6-inch tortillas are wonderfully authentic. Better still, this recipe is not at all difficult to do. If you have kids, it's a blast to include them in the process.

3 cups corn flour or masa harina

1 teaspoon kosher salt

3 tablespoons lard

1 Mix together the flour and salt. Cut in the lard until the mixture resembles small peas. Add 1½ cups water and bring the dough together to form a ball. The dough should be a little wet, but not sticky. Form the dough into balls slightly larger than a golf ball. You should end up with 16 to 18 balls.

2 To press the tortillas, take two pieces of wax paper and cut them to the size and shape of the tortilla press. Open the press and lay one piece of wax paper on the bottom section. Put a dough ball in the center, cover with the other piece of wax paper, and gently close the press until the dough reaches a diameter of 6 inches. If you don't have a tortilla press, you can use a rolling pin. You should press each tortilla just before cooking it.

3 To cook the tortillas, heat a griddle or a large skillet over high heat. Working one at a time, carefully remove the wax paper from both sides. Have the tortilla sit halfway in your hand, so that that it dangles over the side. Gently lay it down onto the dry skillet. Cook the tortilla for 30 seconds to 1 minute on each side. The tortilla should be lightly toasted with small air pockets forming. Remove the tortillas to a kitchen-towel-lined tortilla warmer, or wrap them in a kitchen towel to keep warm. Serve immediately or refrigerate and reheat.

ACKNOWLEDGMENTS

Regardless what you do for a living, you are only as good as the people around you. Fortunately for me, I not only was raised by amazing parents (with great food traditions to boot!), but I also managed to marry way over my head. I'm truly blessed that my wife, Liz, and stepson, Kyle, inspire me every day. Since the very beginning, they have given me the freedom and support to chase my wildest dreams.

I am also grateful to my entire restaurant staff, without whom I'd never be able to work on projects such as this cookbook. Specifically I'd like to thank chefs Derek Clayton, Matt Harlan, James Mowcomber, and Andy Hollyday, who make sure the food in all of our restaurants is excellent while still managing to put up with my quirkiness.

I am grateful beyond words to Doug Petkovic, who in addition to being Liz's and my business partner is also our dearest friend. His continuous hard work and vision is the fuel that runs our company day in and day out. On a more personal level, I couldn't survive without my amazing assistant, Rebecca Yody, who runs my life almost better than me.

Thank you, also, to my manager Scott Feldman and the entire team at Two Twelve Management, Becca Parrish and all the lovelies of BeccaPR, and everybody at ABC and Food Network.

Books, like restaurants, also require a team of people to make them happen. Thank you to Douglas Trattner for turning my thoughts and words into complete sentences with proper punctuation. Thanks to Jennifer May for taking all of these beautiful photographs, many of which were shot during a Cleveland winter while she was six months pregnant. A huge shout-out goes to Katie Pickens, my culinary assistant, who tested every recipe over and over again to make sure they'd work not only in a fully equipped restaurant kitchen but also in your home. I'm also grateful to my editor, Rica Allannic, who always managed to keep me on task regardless of how hard I tried to procrastinate.

Thank you all!

INDEX

Note: Page references in *italics* indicate photographs.

Peach(es)
    & Blue Cheese Salad, 229
    Mint, & Almonds, Grilled
        Chicken Thighs with, 152, *153*
Pears
    Mustard Fruit, 226, *227*
Peppers
    Bucatini with Bacon, Tomatoes
        & Jalapeño, 105
    Giardiniera, *224*, 225
    Habanero Glaze, 81
    Pheasant Chili, Austin-
        Style, *184*, 185
    Slow Roasted Pork Belly Buns
        with Cilantro & Jalapeño, 101
    Spicy Pork Burger with
        Manchego & Poblanos, 72
    Tomato Salad with Red
        Onion & Dill, *22*, 207
Pheasant Chili, Austin-Style, *184*, 185
Pickled Cherries, *180*, 223
Pickled Shallots, *48*, 222
Pickling Spice, 43
Pies
    Chicken Pot Pie, 164, *165*
    Pork, *66*, 67
Pig Trotters
    with Apple & Celery
        Root Salad, 85
    Head Cheese, 96–97
Pine nuts
    Sicilian Cauliflower, 234, *235*
Polenta
    Bacon, & Mushrooms, Crispy
        Chicken Livers with, 143
    Soft, with Aged Cheddar, 248
Porchetta, 69, *70*
Pork. *See also* Bacon; Ham
    Arancini, 102, *103*
    & Beans, 84
    Belly, Slow-Roasted, Buns with
        Cilantro & Jalapeño, 101
    best cooking methods, 63
    Burger, Spicy, with Manchego
        & Poblanos, 72
    Butt, Smoked, with
        Habanero Glaze, *80*, 81
    Chops, Smoked, 73
    Chorizo, 91
    Cracklings, PK's, 82, *83*
    Elvis Biscuits with Pepper
        Gravy, *92*, 93
    Head Cheese, 96–97
    how to choose, 62–63
    internal cooking temperature, 63

Liverwurst, 90
Mussels with Chorizo, 107
Orecchiette with Chorizo
    & Swiss Chard, 104
Pie, *66*, 67
Pig Trotters with Apple &
    Celery Root Salad, 85
Porchetta, 69, *70*
Ribs with Cleveland
    BBQ Sauce, *98*, 99
& Ricotta Meatballs, 106
Shanks, Braised, 94, *95*
Sweet Italian Sausage, 87, *89*
Tenderloin, Grilled, 76
Porterhouse, Broiled, 32, *33*
Potatoes
    Corned Beef Hash, 41
    Spicy Fried, 240, *241*
Pot Pie, Chicken, 164, *165*
Pot Roast with Carrots, Shallots,
    Mint & Lemon, 21
Poultry. *See* Chicken; Game
    birds; Turkey
Prime Rib, 29, *30–31*
Prunes & Macadamia Nuts, Braised
    Rabbit Thighs with, 200

Q
Quail, Grilled, with Citrus
    Glaze, *188*, 189

R
Rabbit
    flavor of, 177
    Legs, Bacon-Wrapped, 197–99, *198*
    Thighs, Braised, with Prunes
        & Macadamia Nuts, 200
Rack of Lamb, Roasted, *116*, 117
Radish, Watercress & Blue
    Cheese Salad, Grilled
    Rib Eyes with, 24, *25*
Raisins
    Sicilian Cauliflower, 234, *235*
Rib Eyes, Grilled, with
    Watercress, Blue Cheese
    & Radish Salad, 24, *25*
Ribs
    with Cleveland BBQ Sauce, *98*, 99
    Lamb, Smoked on the Grill
        with Lemon, Oregano
        & Honey, 124, *125*
    Short, Veal, Braised, 52–53
Rice
    Arancini, 102, *103*
Roasting meats, 27

S
Sage & Turkey Sausage, 169
Salads
    Apple & Celery Root, *208*, 209
    Coleslaw, *45*, 213
    Feta & Cucumber, *218*, 219
    Giardiniera, *224*, 225
    Grapefruit, 214, *215*
    Grapefruit Tabbouleh, 242
    Grilled-Corn, *159*, 217
    Orange, 212
    Peach & Blue Cheese, 229
    Pulled Chicken, with
        Almonds, Apples & Dried
        Cherries, 162, *162*
    Shaved Asparagus, 220, *221*
    Tomato, with Red Onion
        & Dill, *22*, 207
    Watercress, Blue Cheese & Radish,
        Grilled Rib Eyes with, 24, *25*
Sandwiches & burgers
    Fat Doug Burger, 44, *45*
    Lamb Burger with Arugula,
        Feta & Cucumbers, 114, *115*
    Slow Roasted Pork Belly Buns
        with Cilantro & Jalapeño, 101
    Spicy Pork Burger with
        Manchego & Poblanos, 72
    Venison Sloppy Joes, *192*, 193
Sauces
    Blue Cheese, 57
    Chicken Liver, Rigatoni with, 156
    Goat Ragù with
        Pappardelle, *136*, 137
    Lamb Bolognese with
        Cavatelli, 134, *135*
Sausage(s)
    Arancini, 102, *103*
    Chicken & Feta, 168
    Chorizo, 91
    Lamb & Mint, Spicy, 113
    Liverwurst, 90
    Mussels with Chorizo, 107
    Orecchiette with Chorizo
        & Swiss Chard, 104
    Pork & Beans, 84
    Spicy Wild Boar, with
        Cilantro & Lime, 182, *183*
    Sweet Italian, 87, *89*
    Turkey & Sage, 169
    Venison & Dried Cherry, 179
Shallots
    Carrots, Mint & Lemon,
        Pot Roast with, 21
    Pickled, *48*, 222